Freedom Unlimited

Freedom Unlimited

*Liberty, Autonomy, and Response-ability
in the Open Theism of Clark Pinnock*

Jeffrey S. Hocking

WIPF & STOCK · Eugene, Oregon

FREEDOM UNLIMITED:
Liberty, Autonomy, and Response-ability in the Open Theism of Clark Pinnock

Copyright © 2010 Jeffrey S. Hocking. All rights reserved. Except for brief quotations in critical publications or reviews, no part of this book may be reproduced in any manner without prior written permission from the publisher. Write: Permissions, Wipf and Stock Publishers, 199 W. 8th Ave., Suite 3, Eugene, OR 97401.

Wipf & Stock
An Imprint of Wipf and Stock Publishers
199 W. 8th Ave., Suite 3
Eugene, OR 97401
www.wipfandstock.com

ISBN 13: 978-1-60899-469-4

Manufactured in the U.S.A.

Scripture quotations taken from the New American Standard Bible˙,
Copyright © 1960, 1962, 1963, 1968, 1971, 1972, 1973,
1975, 1977, 1995 by The Lockman Foundation
Used by permission.

Scripture quotations marked (NIV) are taken from the Holy Bible,
New International Version®, NIV®.
Copyright © 1973, 1978, 1984 by Biblica, Inc.™
Used by permission of Zondervan. All rights reserved worldwide.
www.zondervan.com

*To my wife, Angie, who has supported and encouraged me
throughout my writing and given me freedom
by calling me to be faithful to her.*

One acts freely in a situation if, and only if, one could have done otherwise.

—Clark Pinnock, *Most Moved Mover*

Human freedom is the God-given freedom to obey.

—Karl Barth, "The Gift of Freedom"

It was for freedom that Christ set us free.

— Galatians 5:1 (NASB)

Contents

Foreword—by Clark Pinnock *xi*
Preface xiii
Acknowledgments xv
Introduction: Beyond Obedience—by Jon Stanley *xvii*

Introduction 1

1   An Invitation to Clark Pinnock 5

2   Freedom as Obedience: The Barthian Response 25

3   Freedom as Faithfulness: "Yes" to The Call of Life 47

4   Power Unlimited: Participatory Freedom 74

Conclusion 99

Appendix: Compatibilist and Incompatibilist Forms of Freedom 103
Bibliography 107

Foreword

OPEN THEISM TODAY OFFERS a fresh perspective on the divine nature which has gotten many people excited again about the doctrine of God. Here in this volume we find a monograph from the Institute for Christian Studies in Toronto which offers a sympathetic critique from a Reformational point of view. Like Open Theism itself, the volume works with the concepts of human freedom and does so with an emphasis on material as well as formal freedom, which is a category needing to be opened up in open theism. Is not the freedom that God longs to see in us more than bare or indifferent choices but loving freedom? Surely God longs not for autonomous selves *per se* but for passionate lovers who belong to his kingdom. This book is not written in a critical spirit but one which issues an invitation to life.

Clark Pinnock

Preface

I HAD NOT INTENDED to write a preface for this work, but it feels appropriate in light of Clark Pinnock's recent passing. I had left the rather apparent meaning of my title for the reader, but now feel that it should be made explicit in honor and memory of Clark. *Freedom Unlimited*, not surprisingly, is an allusion to Pinnock's first published foray into Arminianism in a book he edited, entitled *Grace Unlimited*. This title may be fitting for the theological discussions contained within, but is even more appropriate as a description of Pinnock's presence and attitude toward the world. He was a man of unlimited graciousness.

Because I now live near where Pinnock lived and taught for over 30 years, I often encounter people who are enthusiastic to share their personal experiences of him with me, whether it be as students, fellow church members, or even a few who have been guests in his family's home. The common theme in all of their stories has been an experience of grace. One of the most memorable is someone who, as a student, witnessed a debate between Pinnock and a critic. Even though this critic inappropriately crossed the line into personal attacks, the student remembers Pinnock saying privately that he was happy to have been in discussion and to have had the opportunity to learn for his interlocutor. This is not surprising for those who knew Pinnock, and it is a quality that has been emphasized already in the articles that have been written in his memory.

My experience with Clark was no different. I was only a master's student who, while (clearly, I hope) sympathetic to his position, questioned his definition of freedom. Serving as the external reader for my thesis, his act of grace was to take my work with seriousness and interest, and to later encourage me to pursue publication. Despite the passing of time and complications that made reading and writing difficult, he was kind enough to write a foreword for this work. He approached theological work with a joy and passion that served as a perfect complement to his trademark humility. His willingness to accept human fallibility did not prevent him from taking a strong stand on what he believed to be right—his humility in no way diminished his confidence or passion. I experienced him as a careful reader whose engagement and passion about our shared discipline was contagious. Grace was not an abstract idea to him, it was a way of life.

This work is written as an invitation to Pinnock. I considered changing this both because he had already responded positively (except for some hesitation about my use of Barth, the "theologian of heteronomy") and because I will not have the fortune of further correspondence with him. However, I am certain that his spirit lives in our theological tradition and, though the method of our correspondence has changed, that I will continue to encounter his spirit wherever theology is practiced with grace.

In grateful memory,
Jeffrey Hocking
Toronto, August 19, 2010

Acknowledgments

I WOULD LIKE TO thank my family for being dedicated supporters of my work, I could not have done it without them. I cannot express enough gratitude to my wife, Angie. She has been with me since I began this project, and has encouraged me along the way. My friend Chris Allers, who has been like family over the past several years, has also contributed a great deal to this work.

I owe a great debt to many professors who guided my early intellectual exploration. Among these faculty are: Ronald Mayers, who first introduced me to theology; Dwayne Cole, who taught me to read beyond my perceived limits; and Michael Stevens, who among other things, sparked my interest in Bob Dylan. I owe my initial interest in open theism to John Duff and Jon Hazeltine, who took the time to engage in arguments outside of the classroom. Above all, I would like to thank Matt Bonzo who, in my mind, set the example of an outstanding professor and led me to graduate work at the Institute for Christian Studies.

I have been equally blessed in my graduate studies by faculty and colleagues who have played significant roles in my academic development inside and outside of the classroom. I am especially grateful to my friend and mentor, Nik Ansell, whose careful scholarship, outstanding teaching, and creative thinking have helped shape my theological life. Nik has given me the space and tools to become the student of theology that I hoped to be, and his influence is clear in the best of this work. I would also like to thank Jon Stanley whose outstanding editorial work and insight into this project has contributed greatly to the best of what follows.

Finally, I would like to thank Clark Pinnock, whose work has made this book possible. His determination to remain in the Evangelical tradition as an alternative voice has given many people (including myself) hope that they do not have to walk away from their confession of faith or church because they felt compelled to question theological assumptions. His graciousness as both a scholar and as an individual has inspired what I hope is an equally gracious and constructive response.

Introduction: Beyond Obedience

Jon Stanley

"Your freedom and mine cannot be separated."

—Nelson Mandela

I HAVE LONG BEEN an admirer of Clark Pinnock, the self-styled "theological maverick" who has served as a guide for so many of us that have made the journey to more open styles of Christian theologizing. A generation of younger evangelicals saw in Pinnock a theologian for whom (contrary to many of his critics) being committed to asking difficult questions of his faith-tradition was understood as work of love, and being always "in process" and ever "on the way" was seen as the very heart of the theological task. For those lessons the future of evangelical theology is all the brighter. As Pinnock writes in the Preface to *Most Moved Mover*:

> Over the course of my life as a theologian, I have been a pilgrim and have sought to grow as a hearer of God's word. Theology has been for me a journey of discovery and, though I have respected them, I have not regarded traditional views as beyond reform. One's theology is a work of human construction, even when based in divine revelation, and interpretation requires strenuous effort. Our interpretations are provisional and truth is, to some extent, historically conditioned and ultimately eschatological. . . . An orientation to reform, I realize, does not go down well with those who privilege certain traditions as practically beyond discussion and certainly beyond improving. . . . Appreciation from some and hostility from others comes with the territory.[1]

---

1. Pinnock, *Most Moved Mover*, i.

Needless to say, I was delighted then at the invitation to serve as editor on a project that embodies the best of Pinnock's irenic spirit by Jeffrey Hocking, who has proved himself to be both an astute Pinnock interpreter and an creative theologian (if not a theological maverick) in his own right.

To introduce Hocking's project I will first highlight what I see as three of its discreet contributions to the contemporary theological landscape, before exploring a few of the ways the more constructive side of *Freedom Unlimited*—the invitation to envision freedom beyond the limits of autonomy and heteronomy—could be seen as setting a new theological agenda.

As a study of Clark Pinnock, Hocking has produced a thorough examination of both the theological development and the mature theology of one of the most influential and provocative evangelical theologians of the past forty years. Not only has Pinnock shaped the very ethos of the evangelical movement, lending it a more irenic, generous, and creative spirit, but he has also left his mark on the its theological agenda, being a key player in recent interesting conversations in the areas of scriptural authority, final judgment, social trinitarianism, pneumatology, the divine attributes, (fore)knowledge, and of course, genuine freedom. Honoring Pinnock's influence on a range of theological foci, while focusing on his view of divine/creaturely freedom, *Freedom Unlimited* is among the best of Pinnock scholarship, standing alongside Barry Callen's intellectual biography in *Clark H. Pinnock: Journey Toward Renewal* and Pinnock's colleagues' assessment of his theological legacy in *Semper Reformandum*. Of particular note is the way Hocking brings Pinnock into critical dialogue with other key theological voices, allowing Pinnock's theology to mingle and cross-pollinate with such luminaries as Calvin and Barth, and such interesting contemporaries as Leonardo Boff, Bernard Loomer, and Nicholas Ansell, to name a few. The full tide of Pinnock scholarship is yet to roll in, and we can only hope that when it does it will bring studies that are as incisive, constructive, and far-reaching as Hocking's.

As a study of open theism—the movement the later Pinnock is most closely associated with—*Freedom Unlimited* serves as one of the most evenhanded analyses of the respective positions of both open and classical theists, and what is at issue in the often acerbic debate between them. The amount of straw-manning, *ad hominem*, and special pleading in the literature coming from both sides of the debate is disconcerting

Introduction: Beyond Obedience xix

(and at times misleading), often leaving the reader with the sense that neither side has worked very hard to see the best in their opponents' position. The back and forth concerning God's "glory" is a case in point. The repeated charge on the part of classical theists that open theists minimize God's glory is often lost, in large part because the classical theists fail to acknowledge the different account of glory within the openness position—one in which divine glory and power-sharing are positively co-related.[2] However, while the arguments between open and classical theists often pass each other like ships in the night, Hocking (always the sympathetic reader) makes every attempt to understand each movement on its own terms, and to identify what each movement might have to offer the other, as well as the broader theological conversation. Hocking's own theological journey serves him well here, enabling him to suggest that what is most helpful about the debate is not that a winner is crowned, but that it makes space for further creative theologizing, begging for a theology that is (in some respects) both more open and more classical than either open or classical theism are in themselves.

While *Freedom Unlimited* makes substantive and strategic contributions to both Pinnock studies and the future of the debate concerning the openness of God, it is in his constructive project of developing a new theology of freedom that I believe Hocking makes his most significant contribution to theology today. I say *new* theology of freedom because implicit in Hocking's provocative thesis (that the fullness of biblical freedom cannot be characterized in terms of either autonomy or heteronomy) is the even more provocative claim that the great majority of theological accounts of freedom to date remain within a paradigm that reduces freedom to various shades of either autonomy or heteronomy. Thus Hocking calls for nothing less than a paradigm shift—for new theological wineskins—inviting his readers (lay and professional theologians alike) to envision an account of divine/creaturely freedom that moves beyond the limits (and limitations) of this longstanding and pernicious binary. It is in identifying the need for this shift—echoing (in his own unique way) the still unanswered call to resist both "an empty autonomy and a destructive heteronomy"[3] by one of the theological giants of the twentieth century, Paul Tillich—that Hocking has set an agenda for the theological task as we move into more deeply into the twenty-first cen-

2. See Ware, *God's Lesser Glory*.
3. Tillich, *Systematic Theology*, vol. 1, 86.

tury. In an attempt to make good on the promise of Hocking's project I would like to briefly gesture to a couple of the ways the theme "beyond autonomy and heteronomy" might be taken up in such a theological agenda.

BEYOND OPEN THEISM AND CLASSICAL THEISM

If Hocking is right to suggest that speaking of freedom exclusively in more *negative* terms as the "freedom to choose" (as open theologies tend to do) is ultimately a form of autonomy, and that speaking of freedom exclusively in more *positive* terms as the "freedom to obey" (as classical theologies tend to do) is ultimately a form of heteronomy, then his call to move beyond both autonomy and heteronomy presents a challenge to both theological paradigms. In this way, Hocking's project is a call for better theologies all around, putting the burden on open theists to articulate a critique of positive freedom that does not fall back into "empty autonomy," and on classical theists to articulate a critique of negative freedom that does not fall back into "destructive heteronomy." Even more radical, however, would be to hear Hocking's call to move beyond autonomy and heteronomy as an invitation to move beyond the traditional parameters of the debate altogether, and toward a more comprehensive view of freedom that could be persuasive to both open and classical theists alike.

Taking the biblical account of Adam's naming of the animals as paradigmatic (Gen 2:18–20), Hocking suggests that true freedom is found in our fundamental "Yes" to God's "gift of" and "call to" Life (and thus different from libertarian freedom), but that this "Yes" can be expressed and worked out in a multiplicity of covenantal "yeses/noes" that can be genuinely surprising and pleasing to God (and thus different from compatibilist freedom). In this way Hocking accounts for what might be termed the different classical and openness "moments"—the "Yes" and the multiplicity of "yeses," respectively—in what is a more expansive and dynamic view of freedom, one that includes the freedom to participate in opening up the very conditions of possibility of/for reality (and thus breaking with philosophical realism). Such an account of freedom is neither determinist, libertarian, compatibilist, nor incompatibilist. What makes Hocking's view of freedom so productive then for contemporary theology is that it cannot be accommodated within any of the reigning theological paradigms (Arminian, Calvinist, open, or process), and thus represents what I see as one of the few truly successful attempts to move beyond the boundaries of the current theological discourse on freedom.

BEYOND ATHEISM AND THEISM

Although Hocking does not deal with the topic directly, his project speaks to a particularly crucial area in which Christians today are in need of much wisdom: the question of how to interpret and respond to the atheistic critiques of Christian faith and religious culture. First, Hocking's project lends a needed frame to the debate, allowing it to be understood as for the most part a conversation between the proponents/critics of autonomy and heteronomy. Such a frame is quite helpful, as it positions Christians to take the atheistic critique as an opportunity for self-examination, addressing the plank in our own eye before addressing the spec in our neighbor's (Luke 6:42). The Christian philosopher, Merold Westphal, takes such an approach to modern atheism when he invites his fellow Christians to practice "atheism for lent," allowing the "masters of suspicion" (Freud, Marx, and Nietzsche) to alert us to the way religion often functions ideologically to support psychological immaturity, social domination, and moral self-justification. As Westphal asks, "What if the biblical prophets, apostles, and Jesus himself were the originators of suspicion against the [false] piety of the people of God? What if today's believers should explore the religious uses of these modern atheisms before trying to refute them? What if Marx, Nietzsche, and Freud are plagiarists, who should have footnoted their biblical sources? What if their critiques are all to true all too much of the time?"[4] My sense is that Hocking would suggest that we join Westphal in welcoming the atheistic critique as an opportunity for *metanoia*, allowing the masters of suspicion to point out the subtle and not so subtle ways in which the Christian tradition continues to be characterized by a heteronomous streak that takes a "negative stance toward life"[5] and reduces God's "Yes" to something less dynamic, invitational, and well, interesting. In this way, the atheistic critique could be seen as an ally in the project of imagining Christianity otherwise, that is, a Christianity that is beyond heteronomy and thus at its life-affirming best.

---

4. Westphal, "Atheism for Lent," 71.
5. Nietzsche, *Twilight of the Idols*, 18.

Second, Hocking's project lends to distinguishing among better and worse, or at least more or less productive, atheism(s). In the course of his extended dialogue with the Marxist atheist philosopher, Ernst Bloch, the German reformed theologian, Jürgen Moltmann, came to speak of the difference between an "atheist for atheism's sake" and an "atheist for God's sake."[6] I can imagine Hocking doing something similar, perhaps distinguishing between an "autonomy for autonomy's sake" and an "autonomy for life's sake." In other words, there is a way of understanding the autonomy motif in some forms of modern atheism as a strategic reaction against a particularly closed down form of Christianity, and thus, in its own oblique way a movement towards life. Nietzsche would be perhaps the prime example here. As Nietzsche writes, "The Christian concept of God . . . degenerated to the *contradiction of life*, instead of being its transfiguration and eternal *Yes!*" The so-called death of God then (which had nothing to do with a supposed demise of the God of Abraham, Isaac, and Jacob) is for Nietzsche the negation of the negative, which is why he can respond to God's death by saying, "We . . . feel . . . as if illumined by the a new dawn; our heart overflows with gratitude, astonishment, presentiment, expectation—at last the horizon seems to us again free . . ., at last our ships can put out again . . . , the sea, our sea again lies open before us, perhaps there has never yet been such an 'open sea.'"[7] It might be helpful to hear Nietzsche's response in the context of another line about "the sea" by the German Catholic theologian Karl Rahner: "In the ultimate depths of one's being, one knows nothing more surely than that one's knowledge . . . is only a small island in a vast sea that has not been traveled. . . . Hence the existential question for the knower is this: which does one love more? The small island of one's so-called knowledge or the sea of infinite mystery?" For Rahner, it is the one who ventures out onto the open sea that is "on the threshold of becoming a religious person."[8] Thus in particular atheists we might recognize a certain fidelity to God's "Yes" that is beyond that of the Christian who prefers the predictability of the island to life on the open sea.

Third, Hocking's emphasis on the covenantal dynamics between God and creation would make him suspicious of the monarchical images of God that are often passed off under the banner of theism, and

---

6. Moltmann, "Introduction," 28.
7. Nietzsche, *A Nietzsche Reader*, 209–10.
8. Rahner, *Foundations of Christian Faith*, 22–23.

how such images set off a chain of hierarchies throughout creation. As Leonardo Boff suggests, in much of ordinary theism "God is the supreme authority of the universe, from who all other religious and civil authorities derive, in descending order of hierarchy. As there is only one eternal authority, so the tendency to have only one authority in each sphere of the world is confirmed: a single political leader, a single military chief, a single social leader, a single religious head, a single guardian of the truth, and so on. . . . Much of the atheism of developed societies today is no more than a denial of this sort of authoritarian God and of the patriarchal sort of religion that follows from it and obstructs the development of human freedoms."[9] Boff is helpful here because he allows us to see which "God" is being denied by the atheistic critique. Pinnock reiterates the point when he says:

> We assume in the western world that people know what the word "God" means, whether they believe or not. They think "God" refers, perhaps, to an all-controlling, dominating and aloof patriarch. One's impression of the great atheists is modern times . . . is that they denied an intellectual idol and not the God of Jesus Christ. . . . When they speak about the God whom they reject, I see little resemblance to the God of the Bible, though I do see a resemblance to the God of conventional theism. Atheism is, in part, an unpaid bill of the church which has too often presented God as an alienating substance, remote, unsympathetic, and who exists at humanity's expense. Many of the difficulties with faith are due to problems inherent in conventional theism. . . . The challenge of atheism, and the nihilism that so often accompanies it, is best countered by a clearer vision of God's fair beauty, not by intellectual arguments.[10]

Recently, for theological, political, and apologetic reasons, a host of relational theologians have leveled critiques of the monarchian tendencies in conventional theism by appealing to accounts of the trinity that emphasize relationality, community, and mutuality within the divine life. Thus in their own way such social trinitarians have gone beyond theism (which is not to say beyond Christianity) in an attempt to be faithful to the confession that God is love, that is, a communion of loving persons-in-relation. While Hocking is sympathetic to this "relational turn" in contemporary theology, in the course of his interaction with Pinnock's

9. Boff, *Trinity and Society*, 169.
10. Pinnock, *Most Moved Mover*, 2.

own appropriation of the social trinitarian vision he highlights two ways in which it is still not relational enough.

First, Hocking problematizes the standard account of the two relations in social doctrines of the trinity, suggesting that *periochoresis* (or mutual interpenetration) within Godself does not necessarily translate into a *periochoretic* relationship between God and creation. In fact, Hocking notes how open theism fails to escape many of the problems of conventional theism by leaning on accounts of divine self-sufficiency that continue to position (a self-relational) God autonomously apart-from, and thus heteronomously over-against, creation. As Pinnock writes, "The open view sees God as a self-sufficient, ontologically other trinitarian being. . . . God does not have to relate to some other reality because he is internally social, loving and self-sufficient."[11] For Hocking, however, it only makes sense to speak of God as relational if what we are referring to is the way God is with creation and not simply the way God is with/in Godself prior to or apart from creation. Second, Hocking problematizes the standard account of divine self-limitation in the open theism, arguing that it assumes an oppositional and competitive relationship between divine and creaturely power. As Pinnock writes, "God could have created a universe in which he would determine everything but has chosen not to do so. . . . God made the decision to limit the exercise of coercive power out of respect for creaturely freedom, which, in turn, placed (voluntary) constraints on God's acting."[12] However, according to Hocking, if we begin with a participatory (or nonoppositional and noncompetitive) form of power—in which "God's power does not create powerlessness"(p. 88)—then limitation ceases to be a requirement for power-sharing. If power is participatory rather than coercive, then we can understand God's power as creation's empowerment, and vice versa, and thus mutually generative and genuinely unlimited. Thus, by drawing attention to the *periochoretic* relationship between God and creation, Hocking provides a more substantial critique of conventional theism (and hence a more substantial response to modern atheism) than one finds in standard social trinitarian accounts—going further beyond both atheism and theism (and pantheism and panentheism for that matter) in the name of a more relational theology that might be aptly described along the lines of *covenantal non-theism*.

11. Pinnock, *Most Moved Mover*, 145.
12. Pinnock, *Most Moved Mover*, 147.

BEYOND OBEDIENCE

Hocking's invitation to move beyond autonomy and heteronomy also speaks to how we characterize the very heart of Christian existence. For Hocking, neither a *spirituality of choice* nor a *spirituality of obedience* are able do justice to the fullness and dynamism of biblical freedom. This becomes most clear perhaps in the course of his engagement with Barth. Hocking agrees with Barth that true freedom (which includes both the freedom *from* sin and the freedom *for* authentic human life) is found only in our positive response to God. However, he is concerned that speaking of our response in terms of obedience (as Barth does when he says that "freedom is the God-given ability to obey"[13]) might close down the meaning of freedom by limiting the "singularity" and "multiplicity" involved in receiving God's gift of Life and working out God's call to Live. Taking the narrative in which God is depicted as awaiting Abraham's input on what to do about Sodom and Gomorrah as paradigmatic for "covenantal freedom," Hocking suggests that "*Faithfulness* is a better description of Abraham's relationship to God [than obedience], because he is not asked to answer yea or nay, but is asked for his judgment. Abraham's response is free in that it is beyond either obedience or disobedience" (p. 49). Thus, according to Hocking, "Rather than *obedience* (whether predetermined or not), *faithfulness* serves as a better description of covenantal freedom" (p. 49).

It should come as no surprise at this point that I find Hocking's account of freedom quite winning. Among other things, it has helped me to identify particular areas of my own theological tradition (and all other traditions that give divine law a primary place in our lives and in the life of creation) that are in need of further reformation. Beginnings are important, and it seems to me that beginning with law (as reformed theologies tend to do) is one way of establishing the binary between autonomy and heteronomy that Hocking rightly wants to move beyond. That is, if we hear the Word of Life in terms of law then we are left with the options of either attempting to find our life autonomously "above the law" (and thus in rebellion from God) or heteronomously "under the law" (and thus in submission to God). But neither such a spirituality of choice (in which we determine our own *telos*/good) nor a spirituality of

---

13. Barth, *The Humanity of God*, 82.

obedience (in which our *telos*/good is determined for us) accords with Hocking's view of freedom as faithfulness.

One of the most striking features of Hocking's project is that it even distinguishes itself from the more sophisticated and refined theologies of freedom that still take God's law/order as their starting point, but that attempt to construe such law/order not in a restrictive sense but as being "for our own good" and thus inviting our "willing submission" and "grateful obedience."[14] Such views surely represent a softer form of heteronomy, but the centrality of law/subject relation keeps them from going beyond heteronomy altogether. As Thomas Aquinas writes, "The free man . . . is therefore free not because he is not subject to divine law, but because his inner dynamism leads him to do what divine law prescribes."[15] While such soft-heteronomies are in my estimation the best things going within their particular paradigm, and thus good as far as they go, they remain within a spirituality of obedience/subjection that, in spite of their best attempts to do otherwise, close down what it means to be made in God's image and thus to image God in history. As the Christian philosopher Hendrik Hart says, "It is well known that in human society the more insecure and immature a person is, the less responsibility such a person can assume. This person needs the support of simple and concise rules, of authority, and of decisions which, for a more mature and secure person, would be unnecessary."[16] Thus it seems to me that even the softest forms heteronomy run the risk of underwriting a form of spiritual immaturity that is content to remain being God's servants (merely obeying God) rather than growing up into the responsibility of being God's friends (and thus participating with God). As Jesus says to his disciples, "I no longer call you servants, because a servant does not know his master's business. Instead, I have called you friends, for everything that I learned from my Father I have made known to you" (John 15:15 NIV). That Jesus calls his disciples servants "no longer" implies that there was a time when the servant/master relationship was appropriate. But now that his disciples "will do even greater things than these" (14:12 NIV), "may ask anything in [his] name" (16:26 NIV), and be participants in the Father's will, that time is finished. The new covenant is not a covenant of obedience and hierarchy

---

14. See Spykman, *Reformational Theology*, 249–51.

15. Aquinas, 2 Corinthians, c. 3, lect. 3, as quoted in Congar, *I Believe in the Holy Spirit*, 2:125.

16. Hart, *Understanding Our World*, 302.

but of friendship and mutuality. Spiritualities of obedience, like "spiritual milk" (1 Pet 2:2 NIV), are fitting for a time, but we must not remain fixated with them, as there also comes a time when each of us are invited to go beyond obedience.[17]

Truly going beyond autonomy and heteronomy, that is, living neither above the law nor below the law, requires finding our life in that which precedes and exceeds law (and its corollaries order/ordinance/norm). Hocking speaks of God's "Yes" to life, which is both gift and call, and thus not reducible to a law. Similarly, the Old Testament scholar Terence Fretheim has pointed out that God's first Word to/for creation (the "Let there be" of Gen 1:3) is, despite a long history of interpreting it to the contrary,[18] in the jussive rather than the imperative tense, being more like a divine benediction than a divine command.[19] "In the beginning" was the benediction! Thus the Word of Life comes to us as a blessing rather a law, and blessings do not so much demand our obedience (it would be an odd blessing that did) as authorize and empower our participation. Nicholas Ansell has argued that the intertextual echoes between Ephesians 1:23 (in which God is said to "fill all things in every way") and Genesis 1:28 (in which humanity is authorized to "fill the earth") suggest that, "The human 'filling' of creation, when pursued in covenant with God, thus results in God 'filling' the world with God's presence."[20] Along these lines, imaging God could be thought of in terms of covenantally participating in God becoming "all in all" (1 Cor 15:28 NIV), and the Word of Life could be thought of as the divine blessing that authorizes and empowers our participation. Of course humans can turn a blessing into a law (as even the softest forms of heteronomy do), but that would be to close down the covenantal dynamics of existence, as life in its fullest sense is not a function of our orientation to law (whether above or below) but of the extent of to which we receive, participate with/in, and extend God's blessing.

To head Hocking's call to move beyond both autonomy and heteronomy would revolutionize both our Christian vocabulary and our Christian living, inviting us to move beyond freedom as either choice or

---

17. See Nicholas John Ansell, "Life After The Law?," 7.

18. Cf. Abraham Heschel: "My being is obeying the saying 'Let there be!' . . . What Adam first hears is command." *Who Is Man?*, 97.

19. Fretheim, *God and World in the Old Testament*, 38.

20. Ansell, "It's About Time," 3.

obedience to freedom as covenantal faithfulness, and beyond religion as either independence or dependence to religion as covenantal participation. Hocking's theology of freedom goes hand in hand with a theology of maturity, friendship, authorization, empowerment, and participation, which is why it could be said of those who live into a spirituality of freedom: "They no longer see themselves as servants or children but as God's mature friends."[21] Such is Hocking's invitation to us in *Freedom Unlimited*.

Jon Stanley is a doctoral student in philosophical theology, a practicing psychotherapist, and a theology editor for The Other Journal (www.theotherjournal.com). He is co-editor of *"God is Dead" and I Don't Feel So Good Myself: Theological Engagements with the New Atheism* (Cascade, 2010).

---

21. Moltmann, *Sun of Righteousness, Arise!*, 25.

Introduction

WHAT IS HUMAN FREEDOM? More than a concept, freedom is an idea that reaches beyond our understanding, leading us to an ever deeper sense of what it means to be an authentic individual in the world.[1] Because "freedom" by definition cannot be contained, we must continue to pursue it even as it broadens our horizons of understanding. If our conceptions of freedom become closed, we will have lost touch with what we are trying to understand. This work is born out of that spirit, meaning that it is not intended to settle the argument and define freedom once and for all. Instead it is intended to get what has become a stagnant discussion moving again.

The significance of our image of freedom lies in its location in our web of beliefs. Being close to the center of that web, a change in the concept of freedom means a change in the concepts that flow out of and through it.[2] Understandings of freedom in theological discourse indicate and form the way we orient ourselves to God, to each other, and to creation. Our understanding of the nature of freedom shapes concepts of divine and human responsibility, culpability, and capacity in far-reaching ways. As such, our image of freedom is one of the most significant in and for Christian theology as a whole.

For example, if on one hand, the divine (capacity for) freedom is a manifestation of power, then divine responsibility and culpability will be great. If God's sovereign freedom is a form of autonomy (whether or

---

1. The distinction between "concept" and "idea" is used by the Dutch philosopher Herman Dooyeweerd, wherein a concept is a retrocipation in the foundational direction and an idea is an anticipation in the transcendental direction. Concept is "restrictive" and idea is "expansive." I understand freedom to be an idea because it opens as opposed to a concept which closes (not negatively, but for the sake of comprehension). See Dooyeweerd, *A New Critique of Theoretical Thought*, 2:186–7.

2. I am referring to Willard Van Orman Quine's web metaphor, which he uses to describe the structure of human knowledge (*From a Logical Point of View*, 42–43). This view was popularized in evangelical theology by Stanley Grenz, *Renewing the Center*, 190–206.

not that term is made explicit), it will always be at the expense of human freedom, responsibility, and culpability. If on the other hand, human autonomy is emphasized, then the balance of responsibility and culpability shifts. Both views have important implications in lived experience, especially in the face of evil and oppression. However, both frame the debate in the terms of heteronomy and autonomy and, as such, are only able to shift the balance between one pole or the other. In this case, either divine or human autonomy must be limited. It is my intention to reframe this debate, and my hope is that this book will open a space for constructive discussions about a theology of freedom that moves beyond heteronomy and autonomy.

A recent proposal for a change in our conception of human freedom has been put forward by the advocates of open theism. Clark Pinnock has served as a central figure in this movement, and his understanding of freedom will be the subject of this book. While it is not Pinnock's sole interest, the nature and role of human freedom is a central concern for him as he critically reflects on the assumptions of classical theology. While I believe that Pinnock has rightly challenged "classical theism" and served to open theology in important ways, I intend to argue that he has not (yet) sufficiently opened the true nature of human freedom. My aim is to invite Pinnock (along with other free-will theists) to consider an alternative to libertarian autonomy, which, as I will argue, he believes to be genuine freedom. Contrary to the typical criticisms of free-will theism, a central claim of this work is that an alternative to libertarian autonomy does not necessarily have to limit human freedom. In fact, I will argue that understanding freedom as libertarian—liberty in the sense of autonomy—obscures its true, unlimited nature.

This book consists of four chapters. The first follows Pinnock's theological pilgrimage from his role as a staunch defender of classical theism to his becoming an energetic proponent of open theism. This chapter also serves as an introduction to readers who are less familiar with open theism and its claims as well as defense against some of the unnuanced critiques of Pinnock. It is important in the continuing argument between open and classical theism to move beyond the same points of conflict and the same defensive strategies. An important step in that direction is to reject the arguments that only serve as distractions from substantive engagement.

In this context, I will defend Pinnock's desire to practice biblically informed theology against his critics who accuse him of favoring contemporary philosophy at the expense of Scripture. I find this argument unfair both to Pinnock—because he can only confess otherwise, as he has done numerous times—and unfair to the readers who wish to get beyond shallow critiques to the heart of the disagreement.

For this same reason, I will be careful not to use the word "determinism" to refer to the classical theistic position.[3] Proponents of classical theism rarely claim to be championing determinism; it generally serves as a pejorative term used by free-will theists.[4] A charitable hermeneutic is essential to any good discussion, and if we are to engage in fruitful theological discourse, then we must be willing to hear and respond to the best in each position.

The second chapter follows the development of the concept of autonomy and its association with later definitions of freedom as "liberty." I will argue that Pinnock, who usually does well to question current philosophical assumptions, uncritically embraces this libertarian definition of freedom in his open theology. I will then introduce what I believe to be a unique and viable alternative to Pinnock's understanding of freedom. Such an alternative takes its cue from Karl Barth's insistence

---

3. Determinism is a philosophical position that some classical theists are open to as a normative description of freedom, and I will use the word to refer to that philosophical position. Put simply, this position holds that no act is willed indeterminately; willing takes place within a number of complex causal relationships which may vary in degree. However, in their theology, classical theists rarely refer to God's providence over the world as a form of determinism. Most classical theists would identify this as a philosophical orientation to the world that might describe something true about the world, but not as a fundamental tenet of Christianity. See Helm, "The Augustinian-Calvinist View," 179–82.

4. This is exemplified in a an encounter between William Hasker and Kathryn Tanner. Tanner writes: "God's creative calling forth is indeed unconditionally and necessarily efficacious," yet nevertheless, "my choosing is always a matter of my own inclination, my own tending. My choosing is therefore always voluntary" ("Human Freedom," 114; 121). It is clear that Tanner is advocating a compatibilist understanding of freedom. However, Hasker responds: "When I first set out to write this reply, it seemed obvious to me that Tanner's position . . . is a variety of theological determinism. This still seems obvious to me, but I have learned in the meantime that Tanner does not regard herself as a determinist." This would be well and good, but he continues: "So it is up to me to provide some justification if I am going to refer to her view as theological determinism" ("God the Creator of Good and Evil?," 137). This would be humorous if it were not so frustrating to the reader. Sadly, such labeling is characteristic of both sides of the open theism debate.

that genuine human freedom is found only in obedience. Using this alternative, I will contrast Barth's freedom as participatory obedience with Pinnock's freedom as libertarian autonomy. In my sharpest criticism, I will argue that Pinnock, in making libertarian freedom necessary for love, ends up privileging autonomy over love.

In the third chapter, I will qualify Barth's "obedience" as faithfulness to God's call to/for life. The language of obedience fails to fully express the freedom that is found in faithfulness, not sufficiently honoring the (free) multiplicity of positive responses to the call of life. I will then further qualify freedom as eschatologically-oriented, meaning that the fullness of human freedom is yet to come. If freedom is an eternally fixed amount of power that is merely exchanged and which cannot be created, deepened, or expanded, its distribution will be limited to a zero-sum game in which one can only have freedom at the expense of another. Given an eschatological openness, however, freedom can be thought of as generated rather than merely exchanged. Thus, instead of limiting freedom, faithfulness actually offers unlimited freedom: freedom that is open to/by the future.

The fourth and final chapter will explore the possibilities of an account of freedom as the faithful participation in the power of God. Again, the terms of the debate around God's power have been set around omnipotence or limitation. I find both of these alternatives dissatisfying because they both assume a created (and often fallen) definition of power. Put simply, this definition assumes that power is held "over" (in opposition to) another. Like freedom, power is thought to be a zero-sum game in which one has it only at the expense of another. I intend to suggest an alternative definition of power that is aligned with a definition of freedom as faithfulness. This is a power "for" another that finds resonance in Barth and some process theists.

This alternative understanding of freedom as faithfulness would actually strengthen Pinnock's project, and this critical study is meant as a friendly invitation to continue exploring the possibilities offered by open theism. As we will see, Pinnock desires a theology that is attentive to God's relationality and animated by God's love. I intend to argue that freedom conceived as faithfulness and not autonomy respects such a desire.

1

An Invitation to Clark Pinnock

OUT OF FUNDAMENTALISM

THIS WORK IS A response to open theism as a whole, but for the sake of clarity and style, addresses Clark Pinnock in particular. Pinnock is the focus not only because he serves as a figurehead for the openness of God movement, but also because his own theological development provides his work with a sense of movement. He began his career as a well respected defender of classical theism, contemplated Arminianism for a time, and finally played a significant role in developing open theism. Pinnock is not ashamed to own this development, writing: "I do not apologize for admitting to being on a pilgrimage in theology. . . . We are fallible and historically situated creatures, and our best thinking falls far short of the ideal of what our subject matter requires. A pilgrimage, therefore, far from being unusual or slightly dishonorable, is what we would expect theologians who are properly aware of their limitations to experience."[1] The development in Pinnock's work gives this study a sense of story alongside analysis and exploration. Tracing Pinnock's theological journey allows us to follow the formation of open theism, recognize what is important to the position, and acquire a fuller sense of the theological and spiritual meaning that proponents find in the openness of God movement. Thus, we will begin with Pinnock's "theological biography."

Whether or not one agrees with the direction of his theological pilgrimage, Clark Pinnock has undoubtedly made an intellectually sound and creative contribution to contemporary theology. I have every intention of honoring this pilgrimage by asking Pinnock to journey even

1. Pinnock, "From Augustine to Arminius," 16.

further toward a more liberating view of freedom than that of *libertarian* freedom. But first, we must begin by retracing the steps of Pinnock's journey thus far in order to gain a bearing on where he is now.

As a student, Pinnock frequented an InterVarsity book room in Toronto and immersed himself in the "staunchly Calvinistic writings" of John Murray, Martyn Lloyd Jones, Cornelius Van Til, Carl F. H. Henry, James I. Packer, and Paul Jewett.[2] It was the influence of these writers and the community he sought out in the form of InterVarsity that led him to Calvinism.[3] He writes: "I began my theological life as a Calvinist who regarded alternate evangelical interpretations as suspect and at least mildly heretical. I accepted the view I was given that Calvinism was just scriptural evangelicalism in its purest expression, and I did not question it for a long time."[4] While appreciating its apologetic strength, his attraction to Calvinistic theology was principally motivated by what he felt was its "scriptural" character.

Following Pinnock's career from the beginning, it is hard to deny that his theology is centered around the biblical narrative. At the age of fifteen, Pinnock went to a lecture at a nearby Baptist church and heard a faculty member from McMaster University in Hamilton, Ontario extol higher criticism and its usefulness for biblical studies. Pinnock recalls that he judged the professor's approach as "destructive to our confidence in the reliability of the Bible."[5] His defensive stance toward "humanistic" and "Enlightenment" biblical criticism was only stronger as he finished his theological education.[6] As an evangelical theologian, Pinnock believed his vocation to be the defense of the Gospel against secular humanism and liberal theology.[7] During the formative years of his thology,

2. Callen, *Clark H. Pinnock: Journey Toward Renewal*, 20.

3. Pinnock was not born into a fundamentalistic environment. Interestingly enough, he began going to InterVarsity in order to supplement his attendance of a "liberal" Baptist church which he felt "had forgotten the truth and reality of God." Pinnock, "I Was a Teenage Fundamentalist," 18.

4. Pinnock, "From Augustine to Arminius," 17.

5. Pinnock, "Baptists and Biblical Authority," 193.

6. "Humanistic" and "Enlightenment" are still the terms that Pinnock uses to characterize biblical criticism in the reprinting of *The Scripture Principle*. However, his stance has become much more nuanced and mature in its most recent form. In the most recent edition, he writes: "When criticism comes in, very often faith goes out. It is all too easy to slide from the critical methodology to the critical theology of religious liberalism. Nevertheless, in spite of the dangers, biblical criticism has come to signify many things and many methods, not all of them hostile to the interests of the faith." Pinnock and Callen, *The Scripture Principle*, 2d. ed., 157.

7. As such, it is no surprise that he dedicates his 1985 book *The Untapped Power of Sheer Christianity* to Francis Schaeffer.

this sense of his calling intensified in response to the challenges he saw Christianity facing. No longer did *portions* of orthodoxy need to be defended against certain heretical teachings, but instead, the *whole* of the Christian faith had to be defended against the historical critical method[8] and its attempts to undermine the reliability of Scripture.[9]

In opposition to "liberal" theologians, who attempted to reconcile the Christian faith with the tenets of modernity, Pinnock argued that the two worldviews were mutually exclusive. He writes:

> What is liberal theology? It is essentially a salvage operation, designed to rescue whatever can be saved, after secularism has been allowed to do its thing. It asks, what can we believe now that historic Christianity has been wasted by the acids of secularist criticism? Liberal theology is an orderly retreat from the biblical faith. It gives historic Christianity a decent burial. In order to avoid a direct clash with secularism, the liberals engaged in some crucial cognitive bargaining and agreed to shift to altogether new ground.[10]

For Pinnock, liberal theology was clearly not the appropriate answer to modern secularism.[11] Much of his early career was directed toward fending off liberal theology and modern secularism, and it is important to place him in this context if one is to understand the more militant tone of his early works

As a result of this defensive orientation, Pinnock wrote books with titles such as: *Set Forth Your Case: Studies in Christian Apologetics, A Defense of Biblical Infallibility,* and *Reason Enough: A Case for the Christian*

---

8. Pinnock saw humanism and the dogmatic scientism that comes with it as one of the greatest threats to Christianity: "Christians must not be intellectually intimidated by the church scientific, that humanist-scientist complex which pretends to know everything there is." Pinnock, *Biblical Revelation*, 205.

9. See Callen, *Journey Toward Renewal*, 45–46. Callen gives an anecdote of a 1963 study that "denied the authenticity of many of the letters traditionally attributed to the authorship of Paul." The study relied on computers to perform a statistical study of the vocabulary contained within the letters. Pinnock responded with an article entitled "Honest to Computers?" in the UK edition of *InterVarsity Magazine* (Spring, 1964): 16–17.

10. Pinnock, *The Untapped Power of Sheer Christianity*, 18–19.

11. I use the past tense here, because Pinnock has changed his mind since he penned the preceding quotation. His tone has softened considerably. However, even though he is less militant towards liberal theology now (often being charged as a liberal theologian himself), his core feelings displayed in this statement have not changed significantly. He is still very wary of anyone who prioritizes modern rationality over the biblical narrative; even if it means that he has turned the same critique on fundamentalists as well.

Faith. These works argue that not only are the Evangelical core doctrinal beliefs biblically true, but that they are rationally true as well. Pinnock was certainly not alone in writing rationally apologetic books at this time, but among his contemporaries he was heralded as a leading "conservative voice" following in the tradition of Francis Schaeffer.[12] In his later reflections, he sees his apologetic orientation as an example of the "hard rationalism" of modernity that many fundamentalist critics themselves exhibited.[13] The deep attraction that North American fundamentalist Christians felt for the scientific rationalism that threatened to undermine their faith was an irony that Pinnock later came to appreciate and regret.[14]

The Beginning of a Transition

Pinnock may have begun his theological career as a five-point Calvinist[15] and a rationalistic apologist, but even in his earlier publications, one sees hints of what would become his open view.[16] The 1986 publication of "God Limits His Knowledge" is often taken as the turning-point for

---

12. While reflecting on his early militantism, Pinnock writes: "It may have been the heady mixture of Francis Schaeffer joined to my encounter with Baptist fundamentalism while I was at the seminary in New Orleans. At any rate, in the late 1960s I found myself heralded as a conservative voice, and I succumbed to the populist adulation." In Callen, *Journey Toward Renewal*, 223.

13. Callen, *Journey Toward Renewal*, 229.

14. For a good account of possible reasons for this attraction, see George Marsden's *Understanding Fundamentalism and Evangelicalism*. The fifth chapter entitled "The Evangelical Love Affair with Enlightenment Science" is particularly relevant. In it, Marsden compares the Dutch rejection of enlightenment science by Abraham Kuyper to the American embrace of it by B. B. Warfield. One key (and likely) thesis is that while the Dutch negatively associated the Enlightenment with the French and Dutch revolutions, the Americans positively associated it with the American Revolution.

15. The five points of Calvinism are most recognizable in the English speaking world as the acronym TULIP. They are as follows: 1) Total depravity, 2) Unconditional election, 3) Limited atonement, 4) Irresistible grace, 5) Perseverance of the saints.

16. See Boyd, "Unbounded Love and the Openness of the Future," 39. It is possible that much of his strict Calvinism was tied up in this defense of Scripture, which was very important to Pinnock at the time (and, despite the accusations of some of his critics, still is). If, as a student, he was taught that Calvinism was the only biblically true theological position, then his desire to remain true to the Bible would explain his initial defensive position against anything that put this position into question. This is not merely speculative on my part, for it is clear that his early publications center on the defense of biblical inerrancy and not the compatibility of human freedom with divine providence. Such a reading would also make more sense of his journey toward open theism. While Pinnock may have dropped strict inerrancy, he still held to a very strong view of the scriptural inspiration, and it is this view that leads him away from a compatibilistic understanding of freedom.

Pinnock's journey into open theism,[17] but as early as 1975 he is already wrestling with the evidence of (his understanding of) genuine human freedom and shifting from Calvinism to Arminianism.

In an essay entitled "Responsible Freedom and the Flow of Biblical History," he begins with the simple observation that "Universal man almost without exception talks and feels *as if* he were free. He perceives himself to be a person capable of rising above his situation, of shaping his life and destiny, and making a significant impact upon history."[18] Rather than immediately rejecting this feeling as contrary to doctrine and the biblical text, Pinnock attempts to resolve this apparent contradiction between human experience and his belief that God's sovereignty predetermines history by turning to the biblical narrative itself. He writes:

> When we turn to the Bible, this natural conviction about human freedom is confirmed and strengthened. Man is viewed in Scripture as a responsible agent, created in the likeness of God, who must account morally to his Maker for the way in which he acts and for the decisions which he makes. What stands out in the biblical narrative is not what we might term a "blueprint" model of the universe in which everything is already decided, so that individual enterprises are smothered underneath an exhaustive divine decree (cf. Westminster Confession IV).[19]

Pinnock's later writings emphasize that Scripture portrays a God who is fundamentally relational and thus deeply involved in history rather than a God who foreordains history from a distant eternal present. In his understanding, God is dynamic and relational rather than static and impersonal. It is this scriptural base and existential observation that will later form the foundation for Pinnock's version of open theism.

Contrary to the claims of his detractors, Pinnock makes it clear that he did not begin to question Calvinism because he found it logically unsound, or because he became attracted to the principles of modern autonomy. Instead, he confesses that it was his commitment to Scripture that caused him to question Calvinist doctrines, particularly the per-

---

17. Boyd, "Unbounded Love," 42, n. 10. Pinnock's article "God Limits His Knowledge" is found in: Basinger and Basinger, eds., *Predestination and Free Will*, 141–62.

18. Pinnock, "Responsible Freedom," 95. Emphasis original.

19. Pinnock, "Responsible Freedom," 96. The chapter of the Westminster Confession that Pinnock means to refer to is actually chapter III, which deals with God's eternal decree (chapter IV deals with creation).

severance of the saints. While teaching at Trinity Evangelical Divinity School in 1970, he concluded that this, the last of the five points of Calvinism,[20] could not do justice to—and, in fact, actually contradicted—the testimony of Hebrews.[21] He writes, "Once I saw that, the logic of Calvinism was broken in principle . . . it was only a matter of time before the larger implications of its breaking would dawn on me. The thread was pulled, and the garment must begin to unravel, as indeed it did."[22]

In retrospect, Pinnock's decision to use the word "logic" is unfortunate as it left him vulnerable to critics who, upon his shift to open theism, would accuse him of being more concerned with logical coherence than with biblical faithfulness. However, for Pinnock, it is precisely the failure of Calvinism's logic to adequately engage Scripture that begins his shift toward open theism. Pinnock saw that the internal logical coherence of Calvinism was strong, but this strength assumed scripturally unsupportable claims. The founding principle of Calvinistic logic (at least for the early Pinnock) was that it expressed a biblical logic, and once Pinnock believed this principle to be broken, he began to suspect the fuller coherence.

Pinnock had begun his career countering logic with logic, but became aware that his reliance on logical extrapolation from (what he took to be) the revealed truths of Scripture had eclipsed his ongoing reliance on the biblical narrative. This deeply biblical self-critique can be seen in the shift he makes to a new model of biblical authority. Reflecting on this change in what becomes his characteristic humility and self-awareness, he writes: "I claimed that the Bible taught total inerrancy because I hoped that it did—I wanted it to. How would it be possible to maintain a firm stand against religious liberalism unless one held firmly to total inerrancy?"[23]

Far from representing a higher view of Scripture, Pinnock came to the conclusion that "those who press [inerrancy] hard are elevating reason over Scripture at that point."[24] Thus, in his shift from the self-

---

20. See n. 15 for a list of the five points.

21. As examples, Pinnock first cites Heb 3:12: "Take care, brethren, that there not be in any of you an evil, unbelieving heart that falls away from the living God." Second, he cites Heb 10:26: "For if we go on sinning willfully after receiving the knowledge of the truth, there no longer remains a sacrifice for sins. . . " (NASB).

22. Pinnock, "From Augustine to Arminius," 17.

23. Pinnock, *The Scripture Principle*, 58.

24. Pinnock, *The Scripture Principle*, 58.

described "hard rationality" to "soft rationality,"²⁵ we see him coming to the realization that in the kind of theology he had espoused, a desire for a closed, doctrinal coherence had replaced the ongoing need for Scripture. "In my opinion," he writes, "the desire to have absolute truth is for many evangelicals stronger than their desire to accept the actual biblical witness."²⁶ While these reflections refer to biblical inerrancy specifically, I believe that they also reveal and illustrate the principles that Pinnock follows in his departure from Calvinism.

OPENING UP

Pinnock's initial shift from five-point Calvinism is first to Arminianism, but is not yet a full departure from classical theism.²⁷ As mentioned above, one of the earliest signs of Pinnock's transition from classical theism to open theism (via Arminianism) was in an essay entitled "Responsible Freedom and the Flow of Biblical History." Published in 1975, this piece predates the term "open theism" and any clear or developed articulation of such a theology.²⁸ The major themes of this piece point to the areas in which classical theism is thought to be deficient: freedom, responsibility, responsiveness, and relationality. This essay is significant because it is Pinnock's first published exploration of a well established evangelical alternative to Calvinism.

Response-Ability

An important point of departure from traditional Calvinism for Pinnock in this Arminian phase concerns human responsiveness (what he will later call "response-ability").²⁹ Stating his conviction that the biblical witness is clear that humanity is able to respond freely to God, he writes: "The fall of man into sin through the misuse of the divinely given freedom constitutes an important clue as to the nature of God's rule. For at this point in history

---

25. Pinnock, "How My Mind Has Changed," 237.

26. Pinnock, "How My Mind Has Changed," 237.

27. The most significant departure that Pinnock will make from Arminianism is to reject the doctrine of foreknowledge. See Strange, "The Evolution of an Evangelical," 11.

28. I do not intend to suggest that Pinnock was the first to think this way, but to indicate that it was biblical study (rather than a theological fad) that influenced Pinnock's thinking. This article even predates Richard Swinburne's book *The Coherence of Theism* which Pinnock named as influential in his turn toward open theology. See Boyd, "Unbounded Love," 42, n. 10.

29. Pinnock, *Most Moved Mover*, x.

man *vetoed* God's will, deliberately disobeyed his commandments, and willfully rejected his plans. Like the Pharisees and lawyers later on, Adam 'rejected the purpose of God' for himself (Luke 7:30)."[30]

Pinnock believes that what he takes to be deterministic views of the fall must be rejected because they do not cohere with scriptural examples of humanity's responsibility and freedom. He repudiates the Reformed theologian Loraine Boettner for writing: "Even the fall of Adam, and through him the fall of the race, was not by chance or accident, but was so ordained in the secret councils of God."[31] For Pinnock, this statement is contrary to the biblical narrative and to human experience in general.[32] Not only does Boettner eliminate genuine human responsiveness, but also human responsibility and freedom. Consequently, Boettner's claim also threatens to make God responsible for evil. Pinnock, who himself adhered to Boettner's position at one time, initially saw the apparent contradiction as an "antinomy." In retrospect, he writes that he was happy "to discover that the Bible does not actually teach such an incoherence, and this particular paradox was a result of Calvinian logic, not scriptural dictates."[33]

Pinnock came to see the responsiveness here eclipsed by Calvinism as a central theme of the biblical covenant between God and humanity, going as far as to say: "Evidently God in his decision to create man placed a higher value on freedom than on sinless conformity to his will."[34] This valuation is a result of God's desire to create a creature in his likeness. In Pinnock's words:

> Having called the universe into being, and after creating organic life in plant and animal varieties, God introduced a qualitatively new kind of being—man, a creature who through the exercise of his freedom would be able to shape his own future, a "godlike" creature able to set purposes for himself, to decide and act and achieve, and thus to transform even himself within the historical process.... For man to be created in the "image of God" can only mean that he has been made to reflect the personhood of God and made capable like him of self-awareness, of self-determination and of responsible conduct.... Because of his nature, man

30. Pinnock, "Responsible Freedom," 100–101.
31. Boettner, *The Reformed Doctrine of Predestination*, 353.
32. Pinnock, "Responsible Freedom," 107.
33. Pinnock, "From Augustine to Arminius," 21.
34. Pinnock, "Responsible Freedom," 100.

is the visible representative on earth of the invisible Lord, and is meant to exercise his powers in having dominion over the other creatures responsibly as unto his maker.[35]

Clearly rejecting deterministic conceptions of freedom, Pinnock believes that God created a true covenant partner who is able to respond in freedom and act with authority to shape the future.

Already in 1975, Pinnock argued that classical theism in adhering to a God who is absolutely transcendent (and thus un-relational), rendered humanity unable to respond to God's grace, with the consequence that it was difficult to locate the responsibility (and culpability) for evil anywhere other than with God.[36] Later, in order to surmount these contradictions, Pinnock would come to view freedom as a central analogy between God and humanity: a characteristic shared (though different in proportion and nature) by God and humanity. In this way, Pinnock hoped to emphasize the full human responsibility for evil and to account for a genuine relationship between God and humanity.

Although it is clear for him that humanity is given the authority to shape the future, he had not yet fully realized that he would need to rethink the doctrines of divine omnipotence and omniscience. Emphasizing humanity's genuine covenant partnership that he saw portrayed in Scripture would cause Arminianism to unravel in the same way that Calvinism had for him.

The following chart may help to illustrate Pinnock's movement from Calvinism to Arminianism, and finally to open theism. This three-stage progression is also presented as a two-stage movement from "classical theism" to open theism. This calls for further clarification.

Because Arminianism has become an established alternative to classical theism in the evangelical community (and has become closely associated with open theism for many critics), most would not agree with the following suggestion that forms of Arminianism actually fall

---

35. Pinnock, "Responsible Freedom," 98.

36. The human ability to respond to God's grace is one of the most significant differences between free will theism (both open and Arminian) and classical theism. The disagreement centers around the individual's role in salvation. Classical theists argue that if individuals are able to respond to God's grace, then they play a role in their own salvation, violating total depravity, unconditional election, and irresistible grace (important confessions in classical theism whether or not one affirms the Calvinistic formulation used here).

under the category of classical theism. However, I argue the association is deeper than is normally recognized.

There are some significant similarities between Calvinism and Arminianism that are not shared by open theism. The first is that both Calvinism and Arminianism reject the possibility that God took a risk in creating the world.[37] Yet it is divine risk-taking that becomes important to Pinnock as he continues to wrestle with the problem of evil. While in traditional theism, God either uses (foreordains) or permits (foreknows) evil, both positions are unacceptable to Pinnock, for both hold that God accepts evil to some extent.

The second similarity is that both Calvinism (in holding to God's foreordination) and Arminianism (in holding to God's foreknowledge) are ultimately advocating compatibilist forms of freedom, even though Arminianism is not generally seen as a compatibilist position.[38] Implicit in the open theist position is the conviction that human freedom cannot be compatible with a future which is determined, either through foreordination or foreknowledge.[39] It is noteworthy that Pinnock rejects both Calvinism and Arminianism as he comes to believe that the biblical description of human freedom implies incompatibilism. In the following chart, this incompatibilist view of freedom signifies the point of departure where classical theism (in its broader sense, including Calvinism and Arminianism) ends and open theism begins.[40]

---

37. For example, see the Arminian theologian Robert Picirilli's response to Sanders book *The God Who Risks*. He writes: "What then of *risk*? If one means only that God's offer of grace may be spurned and he may be treaded abusively in work or attitude, then most certainly there is some risk in God's chosen way of give-and-take dealings with other persons. As Sanders says, when he is using the world appropriately, 'God took a great risk in opening himself up to being grieved.' It seems clear, however, that what Sanders generally means by 'risk' *finally and necessarily involves God's not knowing how things will turn out*. . . . Sander's use of 'risk' is predicated on presentism's denial of divine foreknowledge, and in that sense the word is not justified." "An Arminian Response to John Sanders," 489–90. Emphasis original.

38. See Olsen, "The Classical Free Will Theist Model of God," 148–52.

39. It may appear to be a mistake to call the Arminian confession of God's foreknowledge compatibilistic, but it is a merely a different form of compatibilism than that of foreordination. In foreordaining, God ontologically determines the future. In foreknowing, God epistemologically determines the future.

40. A more thorough discussion of compatibilism and incompatibilism as the dividing point between classical and open theism can be found in the Appendix, p. 103.

	Classical Theism		**Open Theism**
	Calvinism ← → Arminianism		*Incompatibilism*
	Compatibilism		
	Foreordination	Foreknowledge	
Divine Sovereignty	God is "specifically" sovereign because God foreordains history, including its specifics. Everything that happens is for a reason. God's knowledge of the future is grounded in God's will for the future.	God is "generally" sovereign because God foreknows history and determines the overall (general) pattern on this basis. This position is usually referred to as simple-foreknowledge.	God is sovereign as the creator of all possibilities. Because God knows all the possibilities, and thus the limited number of actualities, God can approach the world as a master chess player.
Human Freedom	Human freedom is compatible with God's foreordination through an emphasis on voluntarism. Because the will is the center of freedom, as long as it is not coerced, humans can be free. Thus, if individuals desire what God has foreordained, they freely will it.	Human freedom is compatible with God's foreknowledge because individuals are free both to desire and will what they please. God foresees these desires and actions, but does not foreordain them.	Human freedom is incompatible with an unopen view of the future; that is, any view of the future that can be "determined" by foreordination or foreknowledge. Humans are free to create history within the boundaries of created possibilities.
Evil	God foreordains evil as instrumental to the divine plan (whether it be to build character or punish the unbeliever), but God is not responsible for evil in a sinful sense because it is only the human who sinfully wills it.	God does not foreordain evil, but knows all the evil that will take place in history before creation. God's decision to create is thus not risky, but calculated; God knows full well that the evil of history will be overcome by the end of history.	God takes a risk in creating the world with the possibility for evil. As the future is open for God, God could not know if humans would choose evil or not, but had to create the possibility of evil in order to create the conditions for love.

This chart helps to show Pinnock's development and the major differences in each position as he moved towards open theism. Through his pilgrimage, he was able to open up evangelical theology (once dominated by Calvinism) to new and liberating possibilities. Pinnock's central concern was to stress the relational and loving characteristics of God against what he believed to be the overly-transcendent and alienating aspects of God assumed by traditional Calvinist theology. His passion for attending to the biblical witness even when he felt that it contradicted certain Calvinistic and Arminian doctrines of his evangelical community deserves our respect, as does his courage in forging a new theological paradigm beyond both Calvinism and Arminianism.

METAPHORICAL RE-CENTERING: GOD AS LOVE

As Pinnock continued his pilgrimage, he realized that his understanding of freedom would necessitate a re-articulation of the traditional characteristics of God's sovereignty (omniscience, omnipotence, immutability, and impassibility). To ground this re-articulation, he began searching for a root metaphor which he believed to be truer to the biblical narrative. Pinnock's shift to a more metaphorical methodology occurred prior to the publication of *The Openness of God* in 1994. It is difficult to pinpoint his influences in this respect, but it would have been very much in the air at the time that he began exploring open theism. Both David Tracy's *The Analogical Imagination* and Sallie McFague's *Metaphorical Theology* were published in the early 1980s and marked the beginnings of this shift in theological methodology. Terence Fretheim mentions both books as influential in his own discussion of metaphor,[41] and he served as an important influence in Pinnock's thought.[42] This metaphorical shift was important for the openness movement because it allowed critical reflection on the language used for God that had not been possible before.

Nathan MacDonald gives a helpful analysis of how attention to metaphor plays an important role in Pinnock's open theism. He writes:

---

41. Fretheim, *The Suffering of God*, 167–8.

42. Pinnock cites Fretheim throughout his work, once in "From Augustine to Arminius" (26), more often in "Systematic Theology" (118, 122), and then heavily in *Most Moved Mover*. Fretheim does not readily identify himself as an open theist (biblical scholars are less likely to align themselves with theological movements), but open theists have embraced his work on the suffering and relationality of God in the Old Testament as biblical support of their theological position.

> For Pinnock the root metaphor acts as a lens through which others statements about God are seen. Thus Pinnock faces the reader with a choice of models: either God as "aloof monarch" or "caring parent". There can only be one root metaphor. . . . Pinnock argues further that everyone has a root metaphor or model of God. Root metaphors "are the basic portrayals of God which affect how we relate to him." He believes the root metaphor for classical theism has been the image of God as judge or sovereign—legal metaphors. Pinnock argues that this needs to be replaced with an image of God as a loving Father. Further, this metaphor controls the meaning of other metaphors of God, such as God as judge, or king.[43]

Working with a metaphorical methodology allowed Pinnock to work with seemingly conflicting biblical metaphors, making sense of them by privileging one metaphor and understanding all others in relationship to it.

In 1994, he began to use the metaphor of a "loving parent" for God, arguing that such an image makes more sense in an openness model than it does in a classical model. He writes:

> Two models of God in particular are the most influential that people commonly carry about in their minds. We may think of God primarily as an aloof monarch, removed from the contingencies of the world, unchangeable in every aspect of being, as an all-determining and irresistible power, aware of everything that will ever happen and never taking risks. Or we may understand God as a caring parent with qualities of love and responsiveness, generosity and sensitivity, openness and vulnerability, a person (rather than a metaphysical principle) who experiences the world, responds to what happens, relates to us and interacts dynamically with humans.[44]

"God is sovereign in both models," Pinnock insists, "but the mode of his sovereignty differs."[45]

This shift in root metaphors only became stronger in the following year when Pinnock co-authored a book with Robert Brow entitled *Unbounded Love*. In this work nearly every systematic doctrine is revised in light of love. In 1990, Brow had written an article for *Christianity*

---

43. MacDonald, "From Augustine to Arminius, and Beyond," 24–26.
44. Pinnock, "Systematic Theology," 103.
45. Pinnock, "Systematic Theology," 103.

Today in which he observed what he called an "evangelical megashift."[46] Pinnock and Brow subsequently collaborated in an attempt to define what this megashift might be, and determined that it was "an attempt to recover the good news for our time": the good news that God is love.[47]

In Pinnock's next book, *Most Moved Mover: A Theology of God's Openness*, the theme of God as loving Father is fleshed out more thoroughly, particularly in relation to human freedom. For this reason, *Most Moved Mover* is the primary text for our present purposes, and for any reader interested in Pinnock's mature thought. As one of Pinnock's most recent works, it is key for understanding where his pilgrimage has led him.

In the Preface, Pinnock immediately draws the distinction between the all-loving and all-powerful God:

> The open view of God invites believers to consider a new perspective on God in relation to the world. It asks us to imagine a response-able and self-sacrificing God of changeable faithfulness and vulnerable power. It invites us to see God as the power of love that creates personal agents able to freely love him. It is not a naked power. *Love is God's essence and power only an attribute.* His power, however great in physical terms, is an expression of love.[48]

Pinnock finds a point of contact with classical theism by confessing a fundamental tenet of Christian theology: that God's essence is love. Using this point of contact, he is able to challenge doctrines such as foreordination and foreknowledge in the name of a fundamental biblical and theological confession recognized by the tradition. This is one of Pinnock's strongest points, for it is difficult to describe God as a predetermining, omniscient, omnipotent, and especially impassible being when love and relationality become the focal point. For how can a God who is love before all else be a God who does not feel and suffer with creation? Pinnock argues that the heart of the Gospel reveals that God cannot be described as impassable. He writes that "in Jesus Christ we encounter a God who changes for our sake and suffers on our behalf."[49]

---

46. Brow, "Evangelical Megashift," 12–14. This article does not anticipate the upcoming publication of the seminal works in open theism, but it does anticipate an openness in self-identified evangelicals, and thus the climate in which open theism was born into and out of.

47. Pinnock and Brow, *Unbounded Love*, 8.

48. Pinnock, *Most Moved Mover*, x. Emphasis added.

49. Pinnock, *Most Moved Mover*, 27.

The confession that God is love is key to both Pinnock's continuity and discontinuity with classical theism, and thus central (the hermeneutic key) to understanding his open theology.

Trinitarian Love

Like many of the contemporary theologians who emphasize divine relationality, Pinnock turns to the social doctrine of the Trinity (or social trinitarianism) to ground his understanding of love. As Pinnock writes, it is "from the [social] Trinity we learn that the creator is not static or standoffish but a loving relationality and sheer liveliness. It informs us that creation is grounded in God's love and that grace underlies the gift of life itself."[50]

The Trinity, for Pinnock, serves as a way to affirm loving relationship as a primary characteristic of God and to reaffirm the contingency of the created world. While such an emphasis is not unique to Pinnock's theology, it is essential for his account of human freedom, which also finds its source in the Trinity. Our freedom is like God's freedom, and God's freedom is love. Our freedom finds its ground, goal, and character in God's freedom, the true freedom of love.

Trinitarian theology also allows Pinnock to distinguish himself from process theology, which, in its positing of a relational God, requires the eternal co-existence of the world. As Pinnock puts it:

> God freely enters into personal relationships with his creatures, not because he needs to (he already consists of a tri-personal community in which each gives and receives love), but because he wants to since relationality is an essential aspect of God. God does not *need* to create in order to love. He *chose* to create in order to *share love*.[51]

For Pinnock, it is because God is able to share loving relationships as (and thus between) the Father, Son, and Spirit, that world is not a necessary partner. God's intra-trinitarian love is ontologically independent of creation because it is eternal.

God's choice to create is thus made in complete freedom. Here another fundamental distinction between classical theism and open theism

---

50. Pinnock, *Flame of Love*, 23.

51. Pinnock, *Most Moved Mover*, 28. Emphasis added. For a more detailed discussion of how Trinitarian theology distinguishes open theism from process theology, see Pinnock, "Systematic Theology," 108–9.

becomes apparent. Whereas in classical theism the doctrine of creation is thought to be a symbol of God's absolute sovereignty over the world, the emphasis now shifts to creation as the symbol of God's loving nature and desire to share Trinitarian love with an other.[52]

In *Most Moved Mover*, one quickly notices the extensive correlation between love and freedom. For Pinnock, to say that God is Love is to say that God grants humanity genuine freedom. It is because of this freedom—a genuine freedom given to us in and for love—that Pinnock has sought to offer an alternative to all forms of theological compatibilism.

THE FREEDOM OF LOVE

To return to Pinnock's pilgrimage from classical theism, it is helpful to remember that his theological transformation centers on his understanding of God as Love. The significance of this for developing an account of true human freedom is that Pinnock believes that love and freedom are inseparable. In one of his most revealing statements, he writes that in creation "love was the goal and freedom was the means to the goal."[53] It is important to note that by freedom here, Pinnock means *libertarian freedom*: the freedom of the human to make choices for or against God (or love, life, etc.) that are not known by God from eternity past. The creation of genuine love, for Pinnock, requires libertarian freedom in this sense. That said, implicit in this statement is the idea that true freedom finds its goal in love.

It may be helpful to understand the above quotation as an expression of a particular understanding of the relationship between *nature* and *grace*. For Pinnock, freedom (the means) is nature (the created structure of the world) and love (the goal) is grace (that which fulfills and completes nature). Thus for Pinnock, human nature, which at creation is free in the libertarian sense, anticipates the fulfillment of love as grace.

What is important to recognize is that, normatively speaking, Pinnock indicates a movement in history from nature to grace. For hu-

---

52. Pinnock is careful to maintain that creation was an act of power, while at the same time emphasizing that it was also an act of relational self-limitation (Pinnock, *Most Moved Mover*, 31). This is an important balance for him, for if he does not emphasize God's power in creating strongly enough, he runs the risk of being categorized as a process theologian. Yet if power is emphasized at the expense of love, the open position risks slipping back into classical theism.

53. Pinnock, *Most Moved Mover*, 126.

mans, libertarian freedom (the ability to choose for or against) makes way for the freedom of love. In this way (to highlight a distinction made by Irenaeus) we grow from the image into the likeness of God, for whom love and freedom are never separate. Although this is more implicit than explicit in Pinnock's thought, I see the potential here for developing a model of genuine freedom that moves beyond the autonomy implied in the libertarian perspective.

OPEN THEISM AND THE CHALLENGE OF EVIL

As we move into the final portion of this first chapter, I will briefly lay out a few important differences between classical and open theism regarding evil. I will illustrate the former by turning to Calvin as an example of the above-mentioned tenets of classical theology. While many of the compatibilistic understandings of human freedom come from much earlier than Calvin (here Augustine is a seminal figure), Pinnock is particularly responding to evangelicals who find their roots in the Reformation and especially in Calvinistic theology, which makes Calvin a key figure on whom to focus.

Calvin is a careful pastoral thinker when he is writing theology and it is evident from his commentaries that he is thorough in his biblical scholarship. While all theologies are made up of central and peripheral beliefs, throughout the *Institutes* it is clear that some theological categories do not just relativize, but actually displace others. Calvin's understanding of sovereign omnipotence, in particular, leads him to proclaim that God wills evil, including the initial fall into sin. Addressing those who refused to acknowledge that reprobation is concomitant with election and an act of God's volition, he writes:

> They say it is not stated in so many words that God decreed that Adam should perish for his rebellion. . . . They say that he had free choice that he might shape his own fortune, and that God ordained nothing except to treat man according to his own deserts. If such a barren invention is accepted, where will that omnipotence of God be whereby he regulates all things according to his secret plan, which depends solely upon itself? Yet predestination, whether they will or not, manifests itself in Adam's posterity.[54]

---

54. Calvin, *Institutes*, 2:955.

While Calvin may be able to support divine *involvement* in the fall with scriptural resources, the biblical narrative never claims that God is *responsible* for the fall or for the evil which is the result. Placing God in relationship to evil (as the God of a fallen creation in need of redemption) and making it sound as if God is culpable for it (as the God who ordains all things, including evil) are two distinct matters.

Pinnock is right to question Calvin's theological assumptions when they are inconsistent with the full biblical narrative. He reminds us that God weeps with us when we suffer evil, and thus cannot be responsible for ordaining it: "Rapes and murders, for example, are tragedies that make God weep. God did not send them and thus God can be 'a very present help in time of trouble. . . .' Some things are genuine evils: things that should not have happened, things that God did not want to happen."[55] Most Christians would want to confess this, and, to be fair, Calvin did as well, saying that "it would be most unfitting for God to be made the author of death."[56] However, Pinnock finds it equally fair to question how Calvin's contention that God meticulously controls evil for the purposes of bringing about judgment and the strengthening of the righteous does not undercut this confession.

In saying that evil is neither ordained nor permitted by God, Pinnock is insisting on an alternative to the multitude of theodicies constructed in classical theology. Humans, according to Pinnock, are given freedom to do good or evil apart from divine foreordination and foreknowledge, and for this reason they are almost completely culpable in their decision-making.[57] Pinnock's account of evil becomes a more robust form of the free will defense than is offered by Arminians, for God does not even foreknow and thus does not permit (let alone ordain) evil choices. For open theism (unlike Calvinism and Arminianism), God's creation of a free humanity does not entail knowing that creation would fall into sin and suffering.

---

55. Pinnock, *Most Moved Mover*, 47. An Arminian would not be able to make this statement, because if God foreknows all, then all things *should* happen. Here Pinnock, as an open theist, is able to be more sensitive to radical evil.

56. Calvin, *Institutes*, 1:249.

57. "Almost completely" because Pinnock still attributes some responsibility to God via the risk taken in creating free agents: "God knew the creature and is, therefore, responsible for the possibility of evil but not for its actuality" (*Most Moved Mover*, 47). I will address this creaturely responsibility for evil in later chapters.

Pinnock also rejects the notion that all evil is intended for good by God. While he affirms God's ability to redeem evil actions, he denies that there is always a reason for every occurrence of evil (particularly radical evil).[58] Calvin cannot say the same; in fact, for the sake of (his understanding of) omnipotence, he must say that every evil is for a God-given reason of some kind. Evil occurs, for Calvin, either to make the believer stronger, or to torment the unbeliever. In his words:

> Now because God bends the unclean spirits hither and thither at will, he so governs their activity that they exercise believers in combat, ambush them, invade their peace, beset them in combat, and also often weary them, rout them, terrify them, and sometimes wound them; yet they never vanquish or crush them. But the wicked they subdue and drag away; they exercise their power over their minds and bodies, and misuse them as if they were slaves for every shameful act.[59]

Pinnock responds to this sort of theodicy by noting that "Jesus did not attribute things like deformity, blindness, leprosy and fever to the providence of God. He viewed them as evidence of the reign of darkness, which he was engaged in defeating."[60] To be fair, Calvin does not attribute evil to God either; he only argues that it is subject to God's use and control. However, what Pinnock seems to suggest is that Calvin legitimates (and thus justifies) evil in his desire to affirm a divine sovereignty that uses and permits evil. For many Christians (myself included), any justification of evil is unacceptable, even if this requires compromising or, better, re-articulating the concept of omnipotence. One of Pinnock's most important contributions is that he has given many evangelical Christians who take the problem of evil seriously a way to reconceive the nature of God.

The differences that have been cited between classical theism and Pinnock's open theism revolve around evil, in response to which open theism is at its strongest. Classical theism in many ways spoke its last word when it said that God was absolutely omnipotent and thus omniscient. It left itself with nothing to say except to repeatedly attempt to relieve the all-powerful God of culpability for evil by invoking divine inscrutability. Clark Pinnock (for his part) has opened classical theism

---

58. Pinnock, *Most Moved Mover*, 133.
59. Calvin, *Institutes*, 1:176.
60. Pinnock, *Most Moved Mover*, 134.

so that theology has something more interesting (and biblical) to say in the face of radical evil.

An absolute or closed understanding of omnipotence and omniscience has created a blockage in theology, and with its removal we are again free to plumb its depths. However, I believe that an autonomous view of freedom presents another blockage. If we remove this obstacle as well, we may be able to explore even greater theological depths. I invite Pinnock and other free will theists to consider whether the autonomous, libertarian self ought to be a central to freedom, or whether, perhaps, we can conceive of an alternative that will open theology to greater freedom. This is the subject of the next chapter.

2

Freedom as Obedience: The Barthian Response

In the first chapter I sought to honor Clark Pinnock as an innovative and honest theologian whose explorations into the openness of God have given many evangelicals a new way to conceive of the doctrine of God (as fundamentally relational) and the nature of human responsibility (as created co-creators). At the same time, I pointed toward my critical analysis of Pinnock, particularly on the issue of libertarian freedom. In this chapter I will develop this critique, which is intended to be constructive, by bringing Pinnock into dialogue with Karl Barth. Like Pinnock, Barth struggled with the tensions between divine sovereignty and human freedom, but in the context of the theological developments of his day (particularly that of liberal theology and the accommodation of the German Christians), he came to a different conclusion.[1] I intend to flesh out the contrast between Barth's and Pinnock's notions of human freedom in order to better appreciate and critique Pinnock's view of freedom as libertarian.

Both Barth and Pinnock believe that humanity can only experience true freedom in obedience to God; thus this contrast between them must be articulated in a nuanced way, as it often seems that both are working with a similar understanding of human freedom. However, unlike Barth, Pinnock cannot make obedience the center of human freedom because of the way he is intent on setting himself apart from compatibilistic accounts of freedom. For Pinnock *true* human freedom is found (in part) in the ability to say "No" even (and perhaps especially) to God. For Barth, however, *true* freedom is always preceded by the "Yes" of obedience: to say "No" to God is to say "No" to (the source of one's) freedom. Contrasted to libertarian descriptions of freedom, Barth's sentences seem

---

1. Macken, *The Autonomy Theme in the Church Dogmatics*, 22–24.

to end abruptly, as if he omits a clause. For example: "Human freedom is the God-given freedom to obey"[2] and "he [humanity] is free on his side to know God, to obey Him and to call upon Him freely."[3] Read in a libertarian climate such as ours, it is as if all Barth's statements on freedom are missing the "or not" qualifier, as if he somehow ignores the fact that humans often do not choose to obey God. This is what a libertarian view of freedom requires: the ability to obey God *or not* (this is also known as *contra-causal freedom*).[4] However, Barth continually (and quite purposely) omits the "or not" when he writes about freedom. Freedom, for Barth, is always grounded in obedience to God.

Before I delve more deeply into Barth's understanding of human freedom, I want to make it clear that I will later qualify the meaning of obedience. Obedience as traditionally conceived is too closely tied to theological compatibilism, and I intend to open up its meaning in the third chapter of this book. As for Barth's position, I am unconvinced that he had submission to God's predetermined will in mind when he used the word "obedience" and I hope that becomes clear in the following exploration of freedom in his work.

To set some historical context to Barth's reaction against autonomy, I will turn to John Macken's excellent analysis of the theme of autonomy in the *Church Dogmatics*. Macken traces this modern idea of freedom from its beginnings in Kant, via its transformation through Fichte, to its use in the liberal theology that Barth would later denounce.

KANT, FICHTE, AND BEYOND: AUTONOMY IN HISTORICAL CONTEXT

Kant

Kant turns to the autonomy of the will to secure the freedom of all because of his conviction that individual autonomy makes for an egalitarian society. As Macken points out: "[Kant] had inherited from Stoic philosophy the idea of autarchy, that is of rational self-sufficiency and independence on the part of the free individual. However, he reinter-

---

2. Barth, *The Humanity of God*, 82.
3. Barth, *CD*, 3/2:193.
4. Barth uses the term "contra-causal" to describe the account "in which free persons are those who can refuse God." Webster, *Barth's Moral Theology*, 111.

preted the ideal of aut*archy* as auto*nomy*, in which the rational law-giving function of each individual should ensure the harmony of the freedom of each one with the freedom of every other individual."[5] Autonomy as self-rule for Kant is self-rule *for* others, neither apart from nor over against them.[6] For Kant, true freedom could only exist in a society of individuals who are rationally able to understand the ethical imperative. Much like what will be explored in Barth later, autonomy for Kant means *obedience* to the ethical imperative.[7] Ideally autonomy is freedom, but it is freedom for all, not only for the individual. As Macken writes: "Autonomous obedience to universal, rational moral law turns the Stoic ideal of self-sufficiency into the political ideal of the free citizen within the state, whose rational and moral relationship with everybody else ensures the harmony of each person's freedom with the freedom of all."[8]

In order to extend the freedom of one to the freedom of all, Kant maintains a duality between the individual subject and the universal moral law: the universal is always located outside of (or above) the subject, which the subject encounters and in so doing is made aware of his or her relationship to it. According to Macken, this duality is key for Kant in order to curb pure individualism and produce a very different kind of autonomy than that which characterizes contemporary forms of liberalism.

---

5. Macken, *The Autonomy Theme*, 5. Emphasis original.

6. Karl Ameriks makes this point in the introduction to his study of the development autonomy after Kant: "For Kant, our freedom involves a capacity to be not merely an occasional uncaused or self-directed force; above all, it is a power whose action is ever present in an internally generated and law-governed way. The Kantian self is literally 'auto-nomous,' that is, defined by a *self-legislation* that is carried out on itself as well as by itself." Ameriks, *Kant and the Fate of Autonomy*, 4. Emphasis original.

7. While most accept this reading of Kant as true, Herbert Marcuse points out that even so, Kant still assumes autonomous freedom as *a priori* self-determination. He writes: "Freedom for Kant is a transcendental 'actuality,' a 'fact'; it is something which man always already has if he wants to become free. . . . Admittedly freedom 'exists' for Kant only in activity in accordance with the moral law, but this activity is, in principle, free to everyone everywhere" (Marcuse, "A Study on Authority," 141). Thus while Kant maintains that freedom is only in obedience to moral law, it may be argued that he still operates with a transcendental concept of freedom found in all human beings regardless of their relationship to moral law.

8. Macken, *The Autonomy Theme*, 11.

Fichte

Macken places the blame for distorting Kantian autonomy primarily on Johann Gottlieb Fichte.[9] While Fichte ought not to be held absolutely responsible for the path of autonomy beyond his own writing, Macken makes it clear how Fichte opens the way for autonomy to become radically individualistic. Fichte is culpable for his part in the development of modern autonomy when he recenters Kant's dualism, making the subject absolutely autonomous. This is a result of Fichte placing the *Ich*—the Ego—in the position of the first principle of his philosophy.[10] The problem, according to Macken, is that by transcendentalizing the Ego, Fichte opens the possibility for the autonomous subject to be responsible only to him or herself. If moral imperatives are given by the Ego (rather than universalizable moral laws), then what is to prevent the collapse of the subject/object, particular/universal duality and a resulting internalization of ethics? In other words, if the individual contains both the object (Ego) and subject (will) in themselves, what prevents moral relativism?

Fichte argues, however, that his first principle only leads to radical individualism if one identifies the Ego with their own individuality. He goes on to write that those who would make such a mistake are weak in character.[11] Thus, Fichte's understanding of freedom is actually quite similar to Kant's in that freedom is grounded in moral obligation to something that transcends our individuality. However, the important point at which he diverges from Kant is in locating the ground of this obligation within the individual. He writes: "Our contention is not: I ought since I can; it is rather: I can since I ought. The I ought and what I ought to do comes first and is most evident. *It requires no further explanation,*

---

9. Ameriks makes a similar argument in much greater detail. However, Ameriks provides more background by describing how K. L. Reinhold cleared a path for Fichte's assumptions. In regards to freedom specifically, Ameriks argues that while Kant believed autonomy to be morally demonstrable, Reinhold made it a "fact of consciousness" which "is immediately accessible to all and so has a full popular warrant" (Ameriks, *Kant and the Fate of Autonomy*, 151). In other words, Reinhold makes Kant's idea of autonomy that which it was previously not: a dogmatic, absolute claim of individualism. Fichte then criticizes Reinhold's ungrounded assertion of freedom, yet (according to Ameriks) makes an even greater unjustified assertion of freedom (184–5).

10. "First principle" refers to the inexplicable *arche* of a philosophical system. It is the principle that serves as the foundation for all derived principles in a given system. The foundational character suggests that the first principle (unlike those that follow) is neither derived nor available for examination or explanation.

11. Macken, *The Autonomy Theme*, 16.

justification, or authorization."[12] Thus the ought remains, but it no longer requires validation beyond the individual; there is no need to turn to a universal moral law that exists outside the person. The transcendentalized Ego serves as the explanation, justification, and authorization of all ethical ought, meaning that the individual is able to be a rule unto themselves. A psychologically healthy person will live authentically in relation to their Ego and will, always already knowing what they ought to do.[13]

While Fichte may have rid modern autonomy of Kantian duality, he still maintains a dialectical process by positing a teleological (yet unattainable) goal of absolute freedom.[14] Significantly, this goal cannot be achieved individually, for one is always limited by the activity of another. Thus, striving toward the unattainable goal takes place within the human community, intersubjectively.

According to Macken's reading, "ethical progress toward the ideal of absolute self-determination takes place in ethical interaction within this community. If one falls short, the other seeks to raise him to the ideal. In this process the morally better man, Fichte declares, will always win and so society brings about the perfection of the human species."[15] Fichte's modification of Kantian autonomy makes the transition to absolute individualism possible: the person can become a rule unto himself apart from other human beings. However, because he believes humanity to be communal by nature, Fichte never suggests absolute individualism himself. Fichte opens the door to absolute autonomy, but never crosses the threshold.

Post-Fichtean Autonomy

While Fichte was still writing, other German Idealists and the proponents of the French Revolution began to distort his understanding of

---

12. Fichte, "On the Foundation of Our Belief in a Divine Government of the Universe," 23. Emphasis added.

13. Fichte was attempting to make sense of the immediacy of knowing what one must do in a particular situation. Most of us can relate to this sense of "just knowing" what the "right" thing to do is in particular situations. Fichte would consider these people healthy and in no need of Kant's overly complicated description of recognizing moral oughts. For Fichte, a Kantian system would only be needed for people who are mentally ill—people who are cut off from their Ego and a natural sense of moral obligation.

14. Macken, *The Autonomy Theme*, 14.

15. Macken, *The Autonomy Theme*, 15.

autonomy.[16] Macken notes that, while avoiding Fichte's "depreciation of individuality and his pantheist mysticism, [proponents of the French Revolution] made their own selection from his ideas in order to affirm the comparatively simple (and ultimately destructive) concepts of freedom, absolute self-determination and ethical progress that they found in his earlier philosophy."[17] By ignoring the *transcendental* nature of the Ego, which, in effect, fills the place of a Christian divinity for Fichte, those following him (political activists such as the proponents of the French Revolution and philosophers such as Schelling) make the *individual* ego ultimate. Autonomy has now come to stand for absolute individualism and the cultural result was a strong opposition to anything that appeared to be heteronomous (including theism). In Macken's words: "The autonomy theme became a persistent strand in modern atheism: man the subject must be affirmed in opposition to the divine subject that is independent of and superior to man. Here autonomy is understood as autarchy: man is self-sufficient and any point of reference superior to man is excluded."[18] Surprisingly yet significantly, this newly defined autonomy is not limited to atheistic worldviews and is quickly picked up by both Christian philosophers and theologians.[19]

Placing Pinnock

This post-Fichtean climate of autonomy remains with us today and is recognizable in Pinnock's view of libertarian freedom. This is not to say that he simply assumes a post-Fichtean account of autonomy. Instead he combines absolute self-determination with absolute dependence on a divine other. Interestingly, Pinnock seems to rely upon a pre-Kantian ontology (which assumes dependence upon a heteronomous divinity) to found a post-Fichtean autonomy (which rejects dependence upon any heteronomous force). As we will see, this heteronomous deity serves to guarantee our autonomy.

This is a philosophically inconsistent position, for one cannot claim that God is the giver of freedom and yet define autonomy as the ability to reject the source of that freedom. The Judeo-Christian confession

---

16. Macken, *The Autonomy Theme*, 17.
17. Macken, *The Autonomy Theme*, 18.
18. Macken, *The Autonomy Theme*, 21.
19. Macken, *The Autonomy Theme*, 21.

that freedom is found in God cannot find expression in post-Fichtean autonomy, yet Pinnock—serving to represent open theism—attempts to hold the two in tension.

Relying on the theological method of analogy, Pinnock grounds human freedom in divine freedom: human self-determination is like, but not equivalent to, divine self-determination. This combination leads to seemingly contradictory statements such as: "God gives us room to rebel against him."[20] In other words, we are free to determine whatever God has given us the freedom to determine, but Pinnock is not clear whether it is God who gives us the freedom to rebel or whether we have that freedom in ourselves.

For Pinnock freedom is founded metaphysically (our freedom is derived from God) and autonomy is founded via the individual ego (our freedom to say "No" to God is derived from our ability to be a law unto ourselves). While Pinnock is describing something both theologically important and existentially meaningful, I believe he is wrong to describe freedom as (libertarian) autonomy, making it central to theology and necessary for the possibility of love. I agree that God grants humans freedom and that humans make self-determined choices, for such observations describe human life as we know it. However, "self-determined choice" does not adequately name the gift of freedom. Pinnock is pre-Kantian when he locates the origin of freedom in God, but post-Fichtean when he describes freedom as the choice to ignore moral obligation (regardless from where such obligation originates).

In fact, this definition of freedom as self-determined choice is the more vulgar form of autonomy, and would be unrecognizable to either Kant or Fichte. Pinnock's definition of freedom contradicts Kant's definition: "A free will is the same thing as a will that conforms to moral law."[21] Neither Kant nor Fichte describe freedom as the human ability to ignore or reject the ought/law. For both thinkers, the ought makes us aware of our freedom, but our freedom is then only realized when we act in accordance with the ought (not when we act against it). It is his insistence that we can choose against the ought, yet remain free, that makes Pinnock philosophically post-Fichtean. However, it is his insistence that this form of freedom is God-given that makes him theologically pre-Kantian.

20. Pinnock, "Systematic Theology," 115.
21. Kant, *Groundwork for the Metaphysics of Morals*, 114.

Pinnock's position is untenable because our freedom cannot be grounded both in God and in our autonomous selves. We are either free because God makes us free (pre-Kantian) or we are free because we make ourselves free (post-Fichtean). This is one reason that I am dissatisfied with Pinnock's description of freedom, and I invite him and other open theists to further open the possibilities of freedom philosophically, theologically, and biblically.[22]

The open view of the divine/human relationship would be greatly enriched by a more consistent view of freedom which, while attending to the human choice to rebel, also takes into account the freedom one is said to have in Christ: the freedom *from* sin and death and the freedom *for* life.[23] This is more than an argument over semantics—what one calls freedom another calls autonomy. It is a founding theological assumption which has deep implications for Christian thought and life.

Pinnock is quite clear on the point that the source of human freedom is God. However, as I have argued, he assumes a particular form of freedom which if left unexamined will imbue open theology with a particular moral, political, and economic philosophy.[24] It is for this reason that I

---

22. Regarding biblical definitions of freedom, Pinnock often describes two different kinds of freedom, but fails to articulate the difference between them. In his book written with Robert Brow (quite some time after the beginning of his pilgrimage toward open theism), he clearly maintains an association between freedom and salvation. He writes: "Reconciled to God by faith, believers are free of bondage and free to be all they were meant to be. They are justified by faith, sanctified in love and called to a life of hope. Salvation as freedom begins with *justification*, God's acceptance of us despite our sins. The broken relationship is restored, and we are placed on the path to new life. We are freed from the necessity to justify ourselves, since we are accepted freely by grace" (Pinnock and Brow, *Unbounded Love*, 112). It is hard to imagine how this freedom can be compatible with the libertarian freedom which requires the ability to refuse salvation.

23. Arguably a key message of Galatians 5: "It was for freedom that Christ set us free; therefore keep standing firm and do not be subject again to a yoke of slavery" (Gal 5:1, NASB). One of the problems that I will discuss in greater detail later will be the necessary loss of libertarian freedom in the eschaton. Every open theist has this problem: how can we be free to say "No" and still maintain the promise of the eschaton? Paul's statement in Galatians suggests that we will not lose freedom, but experience it more greatly. This is a contradiction between open theology and the Bible that must be attended to.

24. Pinnock is always careful to defend himself against more orthodox theologians who accuse him of allowing philosophy to dictate his theology. In fact, he often turns the critique around by pointing to the Hellenic ideas prevalent throughout classical theism: "The exact relation between ancient Greek philosophy and conventional the-

turn to Barth whose definition of human freedom takes on substantially different content. Ironically, Pinnock praises Barth for breaking free of Hellenistic influences by centering his theology on Christ,[25] yet if he were to follow Barth's Christology fully, I believe he would construct a radically different—and more open—conception of freedom.

FREEDOM FOR BARTH

By the time Barth began writing, the concept of individual autonomy (which by then had matured into its post-Fichtean sense) had deeply affected the climate that Protestant theology inhabited and heavily influenced the liberal theology of the day. During his schooling, Barth embraced this liberal theology until the majority of his professors began to support the First World War. As a result of this, his theology began to take a very different direction.[26] As he writes: "Ever since about 1916, when I began to recover noticeably from the effects of my theological studies and the influences of the liberal-political pre-war theology, my opinion concerning the task of our theological generation has been this: we must learn again to understand revelation as *grace* and grace as *revelation* and therefore turn away from all 'true' or 'false' *theologia naturalis* by ever making new decisions and being ever converted anew."[27]

This radical reorientation led Barth to vehemently reject natural theology, which is most famously demonstrated in his *"Nein!"* to Emil Brunner. It also led his theology to find its center in Christ, from which and from whom his work radiates. Both of these characteristics had a deep impact on what will be the focal point of this chapter: Barth as a theologian of freedom. Both his rejection of the assumptions made by his liberal professors and his focus on Jesus as *the* revelation of God led him to a unique, though not unprecedented, doctrine of freedom.

In his introduction to a collection of Barth's writings, Clifford Green describes how Barth's view was different from his contemporaries:

---

ism is certainly complex, but one does not have to be an expert to sense the significant struggle to align these two orientations" (*Most Moved Mover*, 66). However, Pinnock seems less willing to own up to the philosophical orientation which motivates his defense of libertarian freedom.

25. Pinnock, *Most Moved Mover*, 73–74.
26. Macken, *The Autonomy Theme*, 23–24.
27. Barth, "No!: Answer to Emil Brunner," 71. Emphasis original.

> We must say at once that Barth's doctrine of freedom is not the libertarian, laissez-faire notion that popular culture has adapted from John Locke, John Stuart Mill, Adam Smith and others. Rather, in the tradition of the Bible, Augustine and classical theology, genuine freedom has content; it is not merely the power to choose without any regard for *what* one chooses. Hence freedom is both a freedom *from* evils and oppressions—in a word, sin— and above all a freedom *for* an authentically human life with God and with our human companions —in a word, humanity. That is the import of Barth's reference to John 8:36: "If the Son makes you free, you will be free indeed."[28]

The remainder of this chapter will focus on Barth's doctrine of freedom and how it may be able to speak to Pinnock's open theism in a positive way. I will rely on Barth's work to argue that freedom as obedience may serve as a more helpful model of human freedom for a genuinely open theism than has libertarian freedom.

Perhaps one of Barth's strongest and most succinct statements regarding freedom comes in a later lecture entitled "The Gift of Freedom: Foundation of Evangelical Ethics," where he states: "Human freedom is the God-given freedom to obey."[29] In a libertarian climate like our own this statement might seem totalitarian and oppressive. However, as Barth's doctrine of freedom is unpacked, its liberating potential will, I trust, be revealed.

Rather than a doctrine of absolute human submission, Barth's imperative is grounded in the hope that through obedience, humanity can achieve true freedom. At first glance, this may seem like a rhetorical trick, as if Barth is attempting to disguise compatibilism in more palatable language. However, Barth never uses language that suggests that God *foreordains* humanity's positive and negative responses to the divine call. In fact, Barth calls humanity's refusal of God an "impossibility." He writes:

> Man does actually *will the impossible*. He does actually will not to know God as he might and should know him thanks to the freedom in which the man Jesus does so for him, in the bright light of the existence of this Fellow and Brother. And his thoughts and attitudes and actions express this non-willing, this refusal. He sets himself in mortal self-contradiction.[30]

---

28. Green, *Karl Barth: Theologian of Freedom*, 12. Emphasis original.
29. Barth, *The Humanity of God*, 82. Emphasis added.
30. Barth, *CD*, 4/2:411. Emphasis added.

It would be difficult if not impossible for a strict compatibilist, particularly a Protestant scholastic, to talk about humanity's *willing* in such a way.[31] For Barth, the human is not preordained to remain in his or her natural state of refusal, but actively wills that which is not possible: the refusal of God. He does not suggest that those who refuse God have failed to receive irresistible grace, but that they have chosen against themselves and against God. Barth's view will become particularly important when dealing with the problem of evil, a topic which will be addressed in the following chapter.

God's Freedom

Humanity's freedom, for Barth, is derived from God: God is free *for* humanity (positive freedom). Already Barth's doctrine is substantially different from Pinnock's in that God is not free *from* humanity (negative freedom).[32] It is important for Pinnock to stress God's freedom apart from humanity for two reasons. First, it separates him from process theists who argue that the world is co-eternal with God. He writes: "The openness view asserts that God sovereignly created the world out of nothing and does not exist in a kind of dualistic relationship with everlasting and primordial matter. It denies the process conviction that God is ontologically dependant on the world and that God always has and must have a world to experience."[33] For Pinnock, God's freedom is maintained by separation from and sovereignty over the created order. Creation *ex nihilo* is important to maintain God's absolute autonomy, for any heteronomous substance eternally co-existing with God would im-

---

31. For example, Barth writes: "The electing God creates for Himself as such man over against Himself. And this means that for his part man can and actually does elect God, thus attesting and activating himself as elected man" (*CD*, 2/2:177). A five point Calvinist or even a traditional Arminian would likely not use such language.

32. This is one key motivation of social trinitarians. Because they stress divine relationality, they have to derive a doctrine that allows God to be relational *apart* from humanity, which they find in the ontological Trinity. In this manner, God can be God apart from creation while remaining relational. As Pinnock writes: "Social trinitarian metaphysics (a relational ontology) gives us a God who is ontologically other but at the same time is ceaselessly relating and responsive" ("Systematic Theology," 112). This is a theological move that, while attempting to protect an orthodox doctrine, projects a unbiblical view of freedom upon God. I contend, with Barth, that it is unhelpful to speak of God's freedom *before* creation, because we only know God in relationship with creation.

33. Pinnock, *Most Moved Mover*, 145.

pede God's libertarian freedom. This autonomy acts as a divine attribute for Pinnock: "[God] does not need a world in order to be God."[34]

Second, God's freedom in relationship to the world serves as a model of libertarian freedom for humanity. God's *choice* to create is made in a vacuum. Nothing calls God to create, not even God's own nature which is already "complete and fulfilled." Pinnock writes: "He [God] did not have to create the world to experience relationships of love because he exists as Father, Son, and Spirit. This implies that creation was a free gift and not something that God needed to do."[35] He goes on to write: "It seems that God has chosen to express himself in creation such that creation would mirror God-self back to him."[36] While it may not be Pinnock's intent, this is the freedom we mirror back to God in open theism: the freedom to choose in a vacuum, to choose apart from a relational calling. If God's freedom is *for* anything in open theism, it is to maintain autonomous sovereignty over creation and to establish our freedom in a similar vein.

In contrast, Barth writes that "we may not speak of God's own freedom apart from the history of God's dealings with man."[37] We may only reflect upon God's freedom in relationship to creation. While Barth also grounds God's freedom in the Trinity, he writes that "God's freedom is essentially not freedom *from*, but freedom *to* and *for*. God is free for *man*, free to coexist with man and, as the Lord of the covenant, to participate in his *history*. The concept of God without man is indeed as anomalous as wooden iron."[38] Trinitarian theology, for Barth, is not a way to set God apart as independent *from* humanity, but a way to recognize God *for* humanity. God's freedom is not autonomous choice made in a vacuum. In Barth's words:

> God's freedom is not merely unlimited possibility or formal majesty and omnipotence, that is to say empty, naked sovereignty. Nor is it true of the God-given freedom of man. If we so misinterpret human freedom, it irreconcilably clashes with divine freedom and becomes the false freedom of sin, reducing man to

---

34. Pinnock, *Most Moved Mover*, 145. He goes on to write that "God's nature would be complete and love fulfilled even without a world to love."

35. Pinnock, *Most Moved Mover*, 83.

36. Pinnock, *Most Moved Mover*, 84.

37. Barth, *The Humanity of God*, 70.

38. Barth, *The Humanity of God*, 72. Emphasis original.

a prisoner. God Himself, if conceived of as unconditioned power, would be a demon and as such his own prisoner. . . . In God's own freedom there is encounter and communion; there is order and, consequently, dominion and subordination; there is majesty and humility, absolute authority and absolute obedience; there is offer and response."[39]

Here Barth stands in contradiction to Pinnock, for he is distinctly aware that a theology which purports "naked sovereignty" in God will lead to a mirroring of such in humanity.[40] Thus he warns, "The well-known definitions of the essence of God and in particular of His freedom, containing such terms as 'wholly other,' 'transcendence,' or 'non-worldly,' stand in need of thorough clarification if fatal misconceptions of human freedom as well are to be avoided."[41]

While Barth often describes God as "wholly other," he is also acutely aware of how such descriptions impact doctrines of human freedom. He writes that these definitions "most certainly miss the very center of the Christian concept of God, the radiant affirmation of free grace, whereby God bound and committed Himself to man, making Himself in His Son a man of Israel and the brother of all men, appropriating human nature into the unity of his own being."[42] A theology which maintains the absolute autonomy of God as a central attribute will distort the revelation of God through Jesus Christ and, in turn, distort the divine/human relationship. Unfortunately, though Pinnock's intentions are to conserve an important distinction between Creator and creation, he utilizes the autonomy of God in a way that runs the risk of distorting what has been revealed to us in Christ, that God is always God for us.[43]

39. Barth, *The Humanity of God*, 71.

40. To be fair to Pinnock, Barth does at times stress the self-determination of God, particularly in his earlier works. One such example is found in the beginning of his treatment of the doctrine of election, where he repeats the phrase "God's choice" or "God's self-determination" several times (See *CD* 2/2:54). However, one cannot assume that Barth believes God would choose *against* creation or humanity. While this assumption would logically follow God's choice *for* humanity, I am not convinced it is by accident that Barth never states such explicitly.

41. Barth, *The Humanity of God*, 72.

42. Barth, *The Humanity of God*, 72.

43. The distinction between Creator/creation is maintained in Barth's work. As he writes: "The king does not become his own messenger, and the messenger does not become king" (*The Humanity of God*, 75). However, it is important to remember that Barth writes that God is always *for* humanity. The king is always *for* the messenger. We

38 FREEDOM UNLIMITED

Humanity's Freedom

Having discussed the nature of divine freedom (in both Pinnock and Barth), we are now prepared to address the question of human freedom. The nature of human freedom is always central in theological reflection, and its nature should be discerned in relation to the important issues in our current context. The ecological crisis is one particularly clear contextual example of how doctrines of divine sovereignty and human freedom deeply influence human action. North American evangelicals have been unbearably slow in responding to (if not outright denying) the realization that we as humans may very well be able to obliterate life on this planet. This is due in part to doctrines of human freedom that ultimately relieve us of the responsibility for the world we live in. Paired with an escapist orientation to the world, a theological system that places divine sovereignty over against human responsibility is in a poor position to encourage ecologically sustainable forms of life.

While I would agree with Pinnock that it is problematic when humans are not granted enough freedom in compatibilistic models, I would argue that libertarian freedom is a reactionary alternative which does little to correct the deeper problem of the eclipse of ethical responsibility in the Christian life. To return to the example of environmental responsibility, a definition of freedom that requires neutrality towards God, one another, and the world is no better poised to resist the practice of environmental degradation than a more compatibilistic definition. Wrestling with the concept of human freedom is extremely important when confronting issues such as the ecological crisis. Freedom serves as a foundation for both human responsibility and action in the world.

Barth understands the centrality of freedom for such pragmatic, ethical issues. For him, to reflect on any human characteristic (including freedom), one must always start with Christ, who is not only the electing God, but also the elect human.[44] Jesus serves as the example *par excel-*

---

cannot speak of God's freedom outside of God's relationship to humanity. In his lecture series on Barth, Colin Gunton writes about Barth's struggle to maintain God's otherness from the world without opposing God to the world. He writes that Barth prefers the Latin word *aseitas* (from himselfness) over the term *independentia* which connotes God's opposition to the world. Both words suggest a sort of self-sufficiency, but *aseitas* stresses self-sufficiency *for* the other (Gunton, *The Barth Lectures*, 101). Thus, for Barth, it makes little sense to speak of God's self-sufficiency apart from God's relationship to creation.

44. Barth, *CD* 2/2:54.

lence of true humanity through his obedience and freedom. Through his prayer and obedience —which lead to complete self-giving—he reveals at once both true God and true humanity.[45] Barth describes how Jesus is simultaneously fully free and fully obedient in the following:

> All that man can and will do is to pray, to follow and to obey. The honour of the Son of Man adopted to union with the Son of God can and will consist only in promoting the honour of his heavenly Father. Only as the Son of Man is adopted into this union can He receive, receive His own task, receive the co-operation in suffering which is laid upon Him, receive finally the attestation from above and His own exaltation and glorification. "Not my will, but thine, be done."[46]

Christ, in obedience, brings God and humanity together. While for Barth, the initiation always begins with God, it is not as if Jesus is following a predetermined script:

> The man Jesus is not a mere puppet moved this way and that by God. He is not a mere reed used by God as the instrument of His Word. The man Jesus prays. He speaks and acts. And as He does so He makes an unheard of claim, a claim which makes Him appear the victim of delusion and finally brings down upon him the charge of blasphemy. He thinks of Himself as the Messiah, the Son of God. He allows Himself to be called Kyrios, and, in fact, conducts Himself as such. He speaks of His suffering, not as a necessity laid upon Him from without, but as something which He Himself wills. . . . *In His wholehearted obedience, in His electing of God alone, He is wholly free.*[47]

Jesus the man is Messiah because he completely obeys God, yet in this obedience, he is completely free to act as the Messiah. In this manner, Christ (re)opens the possibility of true human freedom.[48] In obedience, humanity is able to be free.

---

45. Barth, *CD* 2/2:177.
46. Barth, *CD* 2/2:177.
47. Barth, *CD* 2/2:179. Emphasis added.
48. However, as Macken points out, Barth leaves a gap between the freedom Jesus is able to experience as Christ and the freedom that fallen humans are able to experience. He writes: "The difficulty with Barth's concept will arise . . . when he tries to approach the human phenomenon of freedom in its necessary distinction from the freedom of Christ" (Maken, *The Autonomy Theme*, 45). While I agree this is a possible problem for Barth, I wonder if he would argue that Jesus's freedom is found in his full obedience as

Barth, like Pinnock, stresses that human freedom can only be the gift of God, derived from God's own freedom. However, the similarity ends once the content of that freedom is described. Barth writes:

> It is true that man's God-given freedom is choice, decision, act. But it is *genuine choice*; it is *genuine decision* and act *in the right direction*. It would be a strange freedom that would leave man neutral, able equally to choose, decide, and act rightly or wrongly! What kind of power would that be! Man becomes free and is free by choosing, deciding, and determining himself in accordance with the freedom of God.[49]

Thus, for Barth, true human freedom is not choice made in a vacuum: choice without direction. Human freedom is found in answering in a particular direction, in responding not just "yes" *to* God's "Yes," but "yes" *with* God's "Yes."[50]

This definition of freedom stands in distinct contrast to libertarian freedom, which requires the capacity to choose against God and for evil. Barth strongly contends that sin cannot be grounded in the freedom that God gives to humanity: "Sin as an alternative is not anticipated or included in the freedom given to man by God. Nor can sin be explained and theoretically justified by this freedom. No excuse can be provided for sin. In human freedom there is no room for sin by fiat. Sinful man is not free, he is a captive, a slave."[51] Thus, the Barthian response to libertarian freedom must be "Nein!" Libertarian freedom, while understood to be the gift of God, allows humanity to turn away from God. In turning away from God, humanity turns away not only from the source of their freedom, but also from their true humanity. Choosing against God is a simultaneous choosing against freedom and against oneself.

---

a human and thus achievable for all humans as such. In Barth's description of Jesus at his baptism, it appears that his commitment to be "God for man and man for God" is grounded in his humanity which would work to close the gap between the freedom of Jesus and the freedom of his followers. *CD* 4/4:60.

49. Barth, *The Humanity of God*, 76–77. Emphasis added. Note the difference between "in accordance *with* the *freedom* of God" and "in accordance *to* the *will* of God."

50. Barth, *The Humanity of God*, 81.

51. Barth, *The Humanity of God*, 77.

THE LOVE OF FREEDOM

According to Pinnock "the open view of God is about celebrating the loving project that God has set in motion and entered into; it is not about human beings demanding autonomy from God."[52] Yet his understanding of freedom and its relation to love causes me to question whether, for him a loving God can be separated from human autonomy. Pinnock writes: "God [is] a triune communion who seeks relationships of love with human beings, having bestowed upon them genuine freedom for this purpose. *Love and not freedom was our central concern because it was God's desire for loving relationships which required freedom.*"[53] While Pinnock argues that freedom is not the primary concern of open theism, his logic makes it impossible for there to be love without libertarian freedom. If love is primary, if it is God's very "essence," and if libertarian freedom is absolutely necessary for the experience of love, then for God such freedom must also be primary and established in the divine essence.

Libertarian Freedom: Love as Choice

What exactly does Pinnock mean by freedom? It is not freedom itself that is problematic, but the kind of freedom that is assumed. Libertarian freedom is the freedom to choose between options regardless of relational obligations (to put it philosophically: the freedom to choose regardless of causal determination).[54] Pinnock gives his clearest definition of libertarian freedom in *Most Moved Mover*:

> What I call "real freedom" is also called libertarian or contra-causal freedom. It views a free action as one in which a person is free to perform an action or refrain from performing it and is not completely determined in the matter by prior forces—nature, nurture or even God. Libertarian freedom recognizes the power of contrary choice. One acts freely in a situation if, and only if, one could have done otherwise. Free choices are choices that are not causally determined by conditions preceding them.[55]

---

52. Pinnock, *Most Moved Mover*, x.

53. Pinnock, *Most Moved Mover*, 3. Emphasis added.

54. Thomas Pink writes: "Libertarianism says that when as free agents we determine how we act, it really must be we ourselves who do the determining. For our control over how we act to be real, it must come from us, and not from prior causes distinct from ourselves. As free agents, it is we ourselves, and not anything else, who must be the ultimate determinants of how we act. *Free Will*, 81.

55. Pinnock, *Most Moved Mover*, 127.

True to his scriptural commitment, Pinnock bases this freedom in his interpretation of the Bible: "Scripture, like human experience itself, assumes libertarian freedom, i.e. the freedom to perform an action or refrain from it."[56] He also writes: "God granted us the libertarian freedom necessary for personal relationships of love to develop."[57]

Pinnock believes that love is not possible without libertarian freedom —the freedom to say "no." He writes:

> God created the world out of love and with the goal of acquiring a people who would, like a bride, freely participate in his love (Rev 19:7). He could have pre-programmed creatures to love him, but instead created them with the liberty to choose to love him freely. Love was the goal and freedom was the means to the goal. Humankind had to be granted real freedom, i.e. a capacity to respond, if we were to be able voluntarily to enter loving personal relations with God. He values freedom, not so much as an end in itself, but as an instrument to make possible what he really longs for, love. God gives us real freedom because of his desire for loving relationships.[58]

To summarize, libertarian freedom finds its *theological* grounding in the Trinity (as discussed in the first chapter, Pinnock also finds the ground for his understanding of love in the trinitarian relationship), its *biblical* grounding in those accounts which Pinnock reads as consistent examples of humans thwarting God's will,[59] and, as we have just seen, its *logical* grounding as a necessary capacity for the experience of love.

A fellow open theist, Gregory Boyd, explains why libertarian freedom is necessary for true love. He illustrates the deterministic model by picturing a wife who has a computer chip placed in her head which causes her to love her husband without fail.[60] This is the way open theists view compatibilistic models and the only alternative Boyd (and Pinnock) see is a libertarian one. A wife in the libertarian model is always confronted with the choice of whether to say "yes" or "no" to her husband. Adultery and abandonment are the necessary counterparts to a genuine, faithful

---

56. Pinnock, *Most Moved Mover*, 41.
57. Pinnock, *Most Moved Mover*, 5.
58. Pinnock, *Most Moved Mover*, 126.
59. Beginning with the fall, Pinnock systematically reads accounts of humans choosing against God as examples of God-given libertarian freedom.
60. Boyd, *Satan and the Problem of Evil*, 55.

relationship for open theists.⁶¹ These are the only two choices that open theists see: either one is programmed to always say "yes," or one must necessarily have the possibility of saying "no."

Libertarian Freedom as Death

Here it is important to recognize that the freedom to say "no"—to choose otherwise—is not a mere decision between relatively harmless options. The freedom to say "no" (that which makes love possible for open theists) is the freedom to choose *evil*. For those who may not see adultery as evil, a more extreme example may be necessary. The freedom to choose otherwise also involves the choice to commit murder—to be able to say the *ultimate* "No" to the other. A choice against romantic love is not necessarily evil. Many of us have been significantly disappointed or hurt in romantic relationships, yet once time has passed would most likely not describe the experience as *evil*. Pain is not necessarily evil and is, in fact, an important part of life. However, a choice against Love —or against the ultimate calling of the other (beginning with the calling of God) —is a choice against Life itself.⁶²

We only need to consider the first choice "otherwise" given in the biblical narrative to show the consequences of choosing against Love. In the garden narrative, Adam and Eve are told not to eat from the tree in the center of the garden, lest they die (meaning that they would be cut off from the source of Life). Yet they both make a choice for autonomy and in so doing choose against God. In their action they cut themselves off from their relationship to God/Love/Life. The consequences of their choice (the idolatry of the self) is, as promised, death. However, the con-

---

61. I must be careful here to distinguish this analogy as Boyd's and not my own. Certainly within a marriage, saying "no" is necessary to escape oppressive and abusive relationships, but such a situation does not enter into Boyd's own analogy. The choice to say "no" has nothing to do with escaping abuse; rather, the choice not only to say "no," but to commit adultery is that which makes the relationship genuine. The further problem with this analogy is that it falls apart in scope. A wife choosing to no longer love her husband cannot be equated with the choice to say "No" to God—the source of one's life.

62. "Love" and" Life" are capitalized in order to remind us that open theists are not merely talking about romantic love or earthly relationships, but actually talking about our relationship to God. Ultimately libertarian freedom is the ability to choose against God who is both Love and Life. It is much easier to accept libertarian freedom when discussing fallen human relationships, but fallen human relationships are an improper analogy for the divine/human relationship.

sequences of the first choice against Love are not only physical death. Autonomy affects the entire web of relationships including the relationship with other humans (Gen 3:16),[63] with the earth (Gen 3:15, 17–19),[64] and with the future.[65]

It is not much later in the narrative that the choice against Love finds its ultimate expression in the murder of Abel. The choice for oneself, if taken to its end, results in murder, for it is always a choice against another. Ultimate autonomy requires freedom from relational obligations, and thus requires the annihilation of all others.[66] The biblical narrative gives us a much better analogy of the true nature of libertarian freedom than does the wife with the chip in her brain. The ability to choose otherwise is much more serious than saying "no" to a romantic possibility. It is the ability to say "No" to Life itself.

It is not as if I have unfairly introduced the problem of evil into Pinnock's understanding of libertarian freedom, for it is libertarian freedom that founds his theodicy. As he himself puts it:

> God took a risk when he made this kind of a world since freedom entails the possibility, if not the necessity, of genuine evil because love can be refused. Risk was involved in creating this kind of non-divine order because rebellion and defection are possibilities. Evil was not what God willed, though he did make it possible by giving freedom for the sake of love.[67]

---

63. While the curse only directly relates to the husband/wife relationship, it seems foolish to assume that this is the only relationship that is affected. All human relationships are cursed because of autonomous action, and their relationship is one particular example.

64. The vast web of interrelationship—from the creatures to the earth —is swallowed up in the human choice otherwise.

65. While perhaps not explicit, autonomy has closed down creation's future. Future generations will come with great pain, and sustenance in the form of tomorrow's bread becomes threatened as the ground now struggles against humanity.

66. As Rubem Alves writes: "To be alive and conscious is to be permanently involved in a complex network of relationships which are going to condition my being and my behavior. Freedom in the sense of existing outside these conditions, is an illusion" (*Tomorrow's Child*, 103). Freedom will be forever in tension with life if defined as liberty from others. To put it strongly, a libertarian definition of freedom denies life because it is ultimately non-relational.

67. Pinnock, *Most Moved Mover*, 132. As per the discussion above, it must be remembered that when Pinnock is using the word "love" he is not speaking of romantic love, but the Love of God. It is the Love which I have designated by a capital "L" and which is fundamental to life. It also must be remembered that anytime Pinnock uses the

Evil is possible because Love can be refused, yet for Pinnock, this Love can only be experienced as love if it exists alongside the possibility of genuine evil. It is, in the strongest sense of the term, a vicious circle. Genuine evil is not (necessarily) experienced in the pain of failed romantic love. Genuine evil is associated with ultimate choices against the other: rape, murder, genocide, etc. Genuine evil is violence, and it is violence because it is a valuing of the self at the expense of all else. Hence, the choice described by libertarian freedom is the ultimate idolatry: autonomy. This autonomy does not only lead to pain which heals; it naturally leads to death. The choice to eat from the tree in the center of the garden does not lead to death because of some deadly quality within the fruit. Rather, the choice leads to death precisely because it is an act of autonomy.

One can begin to see the quandary that Pinnock places himself in by making libertarian freedom a necessary precondition for love. If God is Love, and the experience of that Love requires libertarian freedom, is God also Choice?[68] Is Love autonomy? Tellingly, evil always follows closely behind choice for Pinnock, which raises the question of whether Love will always be shadowed by evil—even into the eschaton. As Boyd writes: "The possibility of evil is not a second decision God makes; it is implied in the single decision to have a world in which love is possible. It is, in effect, the metaphysical price God must pay if he wants to arrive at a bride who says 'yes' to his triune love."[69] If the possibility of love requires the possibility of evil, how can we hope for love and not evil in the eschaton? I will deal with this question more thoroughly in the third chapter.

If, for Pinnock, Love requires freedom, and freedom is autonomy, and autonomy is an idolatry of the self which ultimately leads to genuine evil, it appears difficult to avoid the conclusion that Love leads to the possibility (if not the necessity) of genuine evil. For Pinnock, the root of the problem of evil lies in his definition of freedom (instead of omnipo-

---

word "freedom," he means libertarian freedom.

68. While Pinnock would never put it in such a way, he does divinize libertarian freedom. This divinization of libertarian freedom is, in part, how Pinnock distinguishes open theism from process theism (Pinnock, "Systematic Theology," 111–2). Libertarian freedom is ultimately God's, for the choice to create was made out of complete freedom. Creation was a choice completely free of relationship and therefore the ultimate act of libertarian freedom. This is opposed to the process position which suggests that the world is necessarily co-eternal with God.

69. Boyd, *Satan and the Problem of Evil*, 55.

tence, which is the root of the problem for Calvinism, or foreknowledge, which is the root of the problem in Arminianism). It is the problem of evil, I suggest, which asks us to question whether human freedom can be defined otherwise, particularly in its relationship to Love/Life/God.

Obedience and Open Theism

I believe that Pinnock and other open theists could adopt something similar to the Barthian doctrine of freedom as obedience without risking what is essential to the position. In fact, Barth's notion of freedom could help articulate a more consistent explanation of what it means for the Christian to be free. However, what I have suggested about the true nature of divine and human freedom does put some of Pinnock's theological tenets at risk. In particular, what I have suggested in this chapter requires a progressive conception of God and humanity's freedom, a relocation of the origin of evil, and an alternative understanding of freedom in the eschaton. While these proposals sound significant, I do not believe that they deviate so far from the openness model that they are incommensurable with its deepest concerns.

In the third chapter, I will flesh out my position so that it is comprehensible and definite in relation to Pinnock's position. I will also open up what I have described above as the Barthian doctrine of human freedom, expanding it from freedom as obedience to freedom as faithfulness. This position, like Pinnock's, will be clearly distinct from deterministic theologies, but without relying upon libertarian freedom. To put it succinctly, I intend to develop a position that is beyond the binary between compatibilist freedom (heteronomy) and libertarian freedom (autonomy).

3

Freedom as Faithfulness: "Yes" to The Call of Life

IN THIS CHAPTER, WHILE remaining in close conversation with Pinnock's writings, I will offer my own proposal for how to best understand the nature of human freedom. At the end of the previous chapter, I indicated issues that must be dealt with if a sound alternative to the libertarian paradigm is to be developed. These include the opening up of Barth's conception of obedience, the relocation of the origin of evil, and the recognition of freedom's expanding, eschatological character. The alternatives I will propose to these issues are not necessarily incommensurable with open theism; in fact, I believe that such a redefinition of freedom along these lines will strengthen the open theist position.

FREEDOM AS FAITHFULNESS: MORE THAN OBEDIENCE

In articulating my own position, I want to make it clear that while I am drawn to the Barthian understanding of freedom (as obedience) I described in the second chapter, I am not completely satisfied with some of its implications. While I do not believe that Barth implied that freedom can be understood as "mere" obedience in his own work, I do think that his claim that freedom is found in obedience is vulnerable to being read as a form of compatibilism.[1] Thus I wish to further qualify my use of Barth's definition of freedom.

---

1. To again turn to Thomas Pink's short, yet helpful definitions: "Compatibilism says that the up-to-us-ness of our actions—our freedom to act otherwise—is entirely compatible with our actions having been all along predetermined by causes outside of our control" (*Free Will*, 18). Pink is here referring to philosophical compatibilism, which may include fate or causation as the outside forces which determine our actions, but the same applies to traditional theism's description of God's foreordination and/or foreknowledge. Pink contrasts compatibilism with what he defends as a better version of freedom, or *incompatibilism*, "so-called because it says that freedom is incompatible with the causal predetermination of how we act by factors outside our control." He goes

A fundamental problem with the language of strict obedience (as a kind of unthinking, undifferentiated submission a heteronomous law) is that it does not fit the model of divine/human interaction portrayed in the biblical narrative.[2] Pinnock is right to point out the biblical passages that describe humanity's freedom in relationship to an open God, and I do not wish to ignore one of the strongest points of his work. Pinnock rejects any freedom that would be "compatible" with determinism as a "freedom only in name,"[3] and he is right to do so. There is no freedom worthy of the name in a deterministic model and my affirmation of freedom as "obedience" is not meant as a return to determinism of any kind. To say that human freedom is found in obedience is to say that freedom cannot be found outside of a right relationship with God, but this should not be taken to imply that right relationship can only be found in heteronomous submission to outside determination.

Right relationship here evokes the language of covenant. Submissive obedience, by contrast, does not allow for a true covenantal relationship to take place. Because covenantal language assumes that both parties are response-able, if one of the parties is deprived of their ability to respond (this being an important dimension of their freedom), Scripture's insistence that the relationship between God and humanity is covenantal makes little sense.[4] Yet this is a deep assumption of the biblical narra-

---

on to write: "Libertarians are incompatibilists who believe that we really are free" (*Free Will*, 13). Thus, compatibilism seems a fair and fitting description of traditional theism (whether it views history as more or less strictly determined), and *incompatibilism* seems to be a good description of Pinnock's freedom as the ability to do otherwise.

2. It should be noted that both the Hebrew (transliterated as either *shema* or *shama*) and the Greek (*hupakouó*) words most often translated into English as "obey" are better translated as "to listen" or "to hear." The choice of this English word by translators can be explained by its etymology. The word "obedience" comes from the Latin *ob* and *audire* (the latter also serving as the root for "audience"), which also implies the meaning "to hear." While "hearing" may be construed as passively or submissively as "obeying," both the Hebrew and Greek words suggest an active role. *Shama* is defined as "hearing with intelligence" and within the Wisdom tradition would suggest a very active and interpretive role for the one hearing. *Hupakouó* suggests a more submissive role (literally "listen under"), but does not absolve the one hearing of the responsibility to discern with wisdom. Both biblical words imply a greater sense of participation and freedom than is often associated with the meaning of the English "obedience."

3. Pinnock, "Clark Pinnock's Response," 84.

4. Pinnock says it well when he writes: "If we are God's covenant partners and co-labourers, it is important that the future not be completely settled, because that would mean there is no room for us to participate in shaping the future in the service of God

tive. To cite one striking example, textual criticism indicates that earlier versions of what is now Genesis 18:22 portrays God "waiting before" Abraham for his response concerning the decision to destroy Sodom and Gomorrah.[5] If God has determined or even foreknown Abraham's response, it seems that Abraham's true ability to respond in a potentially surprising way is lost.

Rather than the language of *obedience* (whether submission to something predetermined or not), *faithfulness* serves as a better description of covenantal freedom. Abraham's freedom in the above-mentioned narrative is not found in merely saying "Yes God;" it is not blind obedience. Abraham negotiates with God, and his ability to respond to God is his freedom. *Faithfulness* is a better description of Abraham's relationship to God, because he is not asked to answer yea or nay, but is asked for his judgment. This is why God is described as waiting to hear what he has to say. Abraham's response is free in that it is beyond either obedience (heteronomy) or disobedience (autonomy).

The question is whether we are faced with a binary opposition between determinist and libertarian understandings of freedom. If we reject determinism, must we thereby accept a libertarian definition of freedom? I do not believe so, and an important goal of this chapter is to argue that there is an alternative to determinism and libertarianism, compatibilism and incompatibilism. Both deterministic and libertarian descriptions of freedom fail to adequately describe the fullness of a covenantal relationship. Freedom is found in responding faithfully, not in the binary opposition between obedience and the possibility of disobedience.

The (Impossible) Anthropocentric Origin of Evil

Perhaps in a postlapsarian world we should recognize libertarian freedom as a part of the human condition, but to see libertarian freedom as belonging to human nature in a normative sense is, I suggest, mistaken. If we are originally given libertarian freedom then we are by nature given not only the ability to choose, but are presented with the possibility of choosing otherwise. In Pinnock's libertarian paradigm, humanity in the

---

as we are called to do." Pinnock, "Clark Pinnock's Response," 151.

5. God and Abraham have been reversed in the Masoretic Text, but the "harder reading" is to be preferred. See Brueggemann, *Genesis*, 168. The New Jerusalem Bible offers one example of Gen 18:22 being translated with this harder reading.

beginning is structurally neutral towards God: we may choose for or against the Word of life. In creating the world in this way, God takes more than a risk that someone will choose evil at some point. The fall is an "accident waiting to happen."

In order to propose that God did not create humanity with the ability to choose for or against their calling (a calling which is oriented toward God as the source of life), I must articulate an alternative understanding of the origin of evil that centers upon the human capacity to create, and not just realize, fundamental possibilities. I owe this reading to Nicholas Ansell, who offers a non-traditional reading of Genesis 3 in this respect.[6] Rethinking the origin of evil has been central to my reflection on human freedom, and the alternative understanding I wish to suggest would be impossible if humanity were not responsible for creating the possibility of evil.

To briefly summarize the key elements of Ansell's article, he begins by rejecting the assumption that the serpent in the fall narrative is Satan.[7] While such a suggestion may initially strike one as biblically impossible, Ansell carefully and convincingly turns to the biblical narrative itself as well as to several commentaries to support his proposal. What such a reading of Genesis 3 allows is an absolutely anthropocentric origin of evil. As Ansell writes: "Contrary to popular opinion, there is no biblical evidence for the widespread belief that Satan fell prior to the disobedience of Adam and Eve. *There is, in other words, no Fall before the Fall.* . . . When we first meet the serpent in [Gen] 3:1, there is no textual evidence whatsoever that anything bad has happened in or to the good creation described in Gen 1–2. To assume that we are supposed to understand a 'fallen angel' in this context is unwarranted."[8]

If there is no fall before the fall, it is easier to locate the origin of evil in humanity, but to make this plausible we must reject the libertarian assumption that God left humanity with a choice in a moral vacuum.[9] Ansell goes on to write:

6. Ansell, "The Call of Wisdom/The Voice of the Serpent," 31–57. One of the important contributions of this reading is that it offers a consistent expression of the Reformational confession of the goodness of creation. This reading presupposes no inherent flaw in the fabric of creation or a fall before the fall.

7. This is supported by the commentary in *The Jewish Study Bible* which states that "unlike some later Jewish and Christian literature, Genesis does not identify the talking snake with Satan or any other demonic being." *The Jewish Study Bible*, 16.

8. Ansell, "The Call of Wisdom," 36–37. Emphasis added.

9. Oddly enough—in contradistinction to his own argument that God ordained the

> If Gen 3 does not present us with the traditional view of the serpent, neither does it lend clear support to the "free will defence," which is probably the theodicy that is most popular with philosophers of religion who aim to root their views in the Scriptures. When Adam and Eve sin, God's reaction is not that of a Deity who knows full well that disobedience is always a possibility with creatures who have been given sufficient autonomy that they may choose to reject God rather than freely love him. . . . Divine incomprehension in the face of evil highlights the fact that the Fall of creation is not an "accident waiting to happen." There is no hint in the text that it is somehow "permitted" (let alone part of some secret divine plan).[10]

In other words, humanity is not dropped into creation with an immediate and undirected choice for or against evil while God looks on wondering what might happen. It is reaching beyond the biblical narrative, not least by speculating before Gen 1:1, to suggest that God decreed the fall as part of a predetermined plan (Calvin does not even seem to suggest this),[11] but it is a similar stretch to suggest that the narrative tells us that God created the possibility for evil.

This idea, that God creates the possibility for evil, is based on (or is the base for) a deprived sense of freedom that Simon Francis Gaine calls the "freedom of indifference." He writes:

> Not only the power to act, but also the opportunity to act are often held to be essential to freedom. . . . Although there is no universal agreement on exactly how to define freedom, of immense influence is the "freedom of indifference": what is crucial to human freedom is not simply that a course of action be the

---

fall (as included in the first chapter)—Calvin's description of the original position is similar to Pinnock's. For Calvin, Adam (unlike his descendants) was given an original choice to remain upright or to disobey God's commandment. Calvin writes that "Adam could have stood if he wished, seeing that he fell solely by his own will. But it was because his will was capable of being bent to one side or the other, and was not given the constancy to persevere, that he fell so easily. Yet *his choice of good and evil was free*" (Calvin, *Institutes*, 1:195. Emphasis added). It is at this point that I would make the same critique of both Calvin and Pinnock (a rare position for Pinnock to be in), as both place Adam and Eve in a morally neutral vacuum. Humanity, in their original state, cannot be created with the choice for or against evil. If they are, evil becomes justified in God's creation of "freely" choosing beings, but this is unacceptable. There ought to be no justification for evil.

10. Ansell, "The Call of Wisdom/The Voice of the Serpent," 45–46.
11. Calvin, *Institutes*, 1:195 and 1:307.

one the agent desires and causes without being determined to do so, but that the agent has chosen it from among alternative choices of action. Freedom of will comes down to choice, and the freedom of indifference means that each course of action is a genuine possibility for the will's choice.[12]

This denatured sense of freedom (as indifference) operates as a fundamental presupposition in the libertarian paradigm, and often goes unquestioned because it is so deeply imbedded in our modern, Western culture. As Genesis does not suggest that God places man and woman in a position of moral indifference, to uncritically accept this libertarian model of freedom is philosophically and theologically irresponsible.[13]

One might counter this claim by arguing that the prohibition against eating in the center of the garden presupposes human autonomy and neutrality which is here being put to the test. But this would involve a reading which is not supported by the Genesis narrative itself. God's prohibition does not have to be understood as a test at all. It only appears to present us with an alternative between eating and not eating after the fall, but it is possible to read the prohibition as a warning which does not *expect* trespass: a warning for humanity's "own good." In other words, God tells the human couple not to eat from the tree not to test their obedience, but because God knows that it will bring death.

Parents often give such warnings to their children. These warnings do not assume that children may be disobedient, only that they do not possess the maturity to understand the danger. I remember a time as a child in which my mother warned me not to touch the curling iron be-

---

12. Gaine, *Will There Be Free Will In Heaven?*, 12.

13. Whether or not one agrees with Marx's utopian vision, his critique of the depraved understanding of humanity in liberalism is quite startling. He writes: "What constitutes liberty? . . . It is a question of the liberty of man regarded as an isolated monad, withdrawn into himself . . . not founded upon the relations between man and man, but rather upon the separation of man from man. . . . None of the supposed rights of man, therefore, go beyond the egoistic man. . . . The only bond between men is natural necessity, need and private interest, the preservation of their property and their egoistic persons" (Marx, "On the Jewish Question," 42–43).

I would not proclaim that the Marxist anthropology is *the* Christian understanding of humanity, however, there is no reason to assume that the anthropology of liberalism is any better. I believe that both are deficient to some extent, but find it necessary to be critical of the way liberal anthropology (and the definition of freedom that follows) has been and still is assumed by North American evangelical theologians. We should be careful not to assume that we have reached "the end of history" and that liberalism (as the philosophy of autonomous individualism) has won the day.

cause it was hot. She did not make this prohibition because she expected or suspected my disobedience, and her surprise after I did grab it suggests that my disobedience never even crossed her mind. My mother's warning only assumed my immaturity and my inability to recognize the danger. It was not as if the prohibition against touching the curling iron was a test of my obedience or love for her. Similarly, the Genesis prohibition makes more sense as a warning considering the newly created humans' immaturity (meaning that they were meant to grow in wisdom, once again, from image to likeness) than as a test of their obedience or love for God. God did not expect them to eat from the tree any more than my mother expected me to grab the curling iron.

Unfortunately, Pinnock's reading of the fall (and the falls that continue to take place as a result) assumes that humans were created with a moral choice for or against God. He writes:

> God sovereignly decided to create a world containing morally free beings who had the possibility of serving God or not. This was something for them to decide such that sin was a *possibility*, though not a certainty, at the time of creation. God knew the creature and is, therefore, responsible for the *possibility of evil* but not for its actuality. It is a good thing for us to have the freedom to choose between good and evil, even though it entails the possibility of making wrong choices.[14]

To assume that even the possibility for evil was created by God (for whatever reason), is to read *against* the Genesis narrative. Pinnock often makes the point that God is genuinely surprised by humanity's disobedience, but he does not take this surprise seriously enough.[15]

Original creation does not have to be understood as some sort of testing ground in which man and woman are given the choice for or against God. Instead, I believe that humans are originally created in right relationship with God rather than in a state that is structurally neutral towards God. It is possible to remain true to the biblical story and say that God never saw the fall coming. This means that evil is not a possibil-

---

14. Pinnock, *Most Moved Mover*, 47. Emphasis added.

15. Pinnock, "Systematic Theology," 123. God's surprise by the future (in this case, humanity's choice for evil) is an opening in Pinnock's theology which suggests that he may be willing to hear my critique. If God did set the tree in the middle of the garden as a test (or a way for humanity to exhibit their libertarian freedom), then it seems God would have been angry *before* being surprised.

ity given in the original creation; rather, humanity *creates the possibility* in their unforeseen disobedience.[16]

The human creation of possibilities breaks not only with classical theism, but also with the Western tradition of philosophical realism, for it claims that possibility does not always precede actuality, but that possibility may be created in the actuality of an event.[17] This is what the pragmatist philosopher Roberto Unger means when, criticizing what he describes as the philosophical tradition's "spectral" understanding of possibility, he claims that "the possible is not the antecedent of the actual but its consequence."[18] He goes on to write:

> Something new has emerged in the world, something we may have ourselves created. It may have arisen in violation of the rules

---

16. Such a proposal puts omnipotence and omniscience into question, but not much farther than Pinnock's own challenges to these Greek categories. While my understanding of omnipotence differs from Pinnock's, I will save that discussion for the fourth chapter. I will say that I do not believe that God foresees *all possibilities*, because I do not believe that God foresaw the possibility of evil. Humanity is *completely* responsible for the origins of evil, and that includes their creation of the possibility. Pinnock writes that "God as temporal knows the world successively and does not know future acts, which are freely chosen in a libertarian sense. The absence of such knowledge does not negate God's omniscience because he still knows every possible choice and every possible consequence of it" (*Most Moved Mover*, 101). While I am not convinced that it is worth defending such extra-biblical categories, I will argue that my understanding of the fall does not necessarily detract from God's omniscience either. My argument only goes one step further to suggest that God, having given humans power to create new and surprising possibilities (though not in a libertarian sense), cannot know all future possibilities. However, God still knows all that can be known.

17. Realism is a philosophical attempt to limit the conditions of possibility through rationality. Thanks to the memorable title of Alasdair MacIntyre's 1988 book, students of moral philosophy will reflexively ask: "Which rationality?" Rubem Alves argues that what is accepted as rationally possible is determined by the structures of power in any given society. In such a society, the powerful are compelled to sustain a particular rationality for the sake of remaining in power (even if they themselves are enslaved by it). If the conditions of possibility were to change, their position in society would also be subject to change. Realism serves to protect the structures of power by marginalizing any changes in the conditions of possibility. Jesus's teachings about the Kingdom of God offer a powerful example of this. He suggested that the meek would inherit the earth, that the first would be last, and he was able to forgive sins and make God present in the world (functions previously limited to the temple). These suggested serious changes in the conditions of possibility and had to be silenced by those in power. However, the resurrection serves as a promise that the power structures of the day and the realism that protects them do not have the last word. For Alves's discussion of realism, see *Tomorrow's Child*, 1–58.

18. Unger, *The Self Awakened*, 61.

of possibility and propriety codified in the preexisting regimes of society or thought. We then rearrange our view of the constraints on the transformation of certain pieces of the world. This rearrangement is our image of the possible. Correctly understood, it is an afterglow that we now mistake for an antecedent light.[19]

This is what I mean when I write that humanity created the possibility of evil: the possibility is the afterglow of the actuality of our disobedience, not its antecedent light.

This coheres with Ansell's claim that in Genesis: "The origin of evil is deeply mysterious, as evil has no legitimate place in the order of things.... What we are actually told [in Genesis], I suggest is that human beings alone *are responsible* for the historical origins of evil, while God *takes responsibility* for liberating us and the rest of creation from the effects of our disobedience."[20] Locating the origin of evil in humanity alone opens up the possibility for a redefinition of freedom that is far more radical and biblical than Pinnock's libertarian challenge to classical theism. However, while I may be taking divine omnipotence one step farther away from the traditional description, it is my hope that I am being true to Pinnock's desire to absolve God of culpability for the creation of evil. Eliminating God's responsibility for creating the possibility of evil offers the open position greater consistency. It also expands open theism's understanding of our responsibility for the direction of history as created co-creators.[21]

God-given Freedom

If the possibility of/for evil is not a part of the originally created human condition, then how do can we account for the reality of genuine human freedom? For Pinnock, the possibility to choose *against* God is a necessary condition for freedom (and love), so if God did not create

19. Unger, *The Self Awakened*, 61.
20. Ansell, "The Call of Wisdom," 46. Emphasis original.
21. I diverge from Barth at this point as well, for while he maintained a very strong position on human freedom, I do not believe he allows for the human creation of possibilities. Macken writes that later in the *Church Dogmatics* Barth "affirms a real distinction between the action of God and human action. The human being has a proper sphere of activity. But this is admitted at the cost of allowing nothing of ultimate significance to happen within this sphere" (*The Autonomy Theme*, 181). I affirm Barth's desire to ground all human action in God, but I believe that this ought not limit the human's co-creational possibilities.

this possibility, how can humanity be free? While I have already argued that freedom is available to humanity through obedience, how can I still call this freedom without falling into compatibilism? Because, as I will argue below, the form of "obedience" I am advocating is not a matter of answering submissively to divine directives.

Like Pinnock, I wish to affirm that God wishes to be surprised by creation and offers men and women true freedom to this end.[22] As Pinnock writes, freedom means that: "God created a dynamic and changing world and enjoys getting to know it. It is a world of freedom, capable of genuine novelty, inexhaustible creativity and real surprises. I believe that God takes delight in the spontaneity of the universe and enjoys continuing to get to know it in a love that never changes, just as we love to get to know our children as they grow up."[23] However, I contend that this freedom can only be realized by human choice *for* God. To speak only of choice *for* does not necessarily limit possibilities. I am thinking particularly of the first task given to Adam (other than to respond by breathing): to name the creatures God has created. It is written that God brought the creatures before Adam "to see what he would call them" (Gen 2:19). God did not bring the creatures before Adam to see whether or not he would name them (as a libertarian understanding of freedom might suggest), but to see (and be surprised by) how he would name them. Adam's freedom is found in the act of naming, not in the choice whether or not to name. His freedom, in other words, is in relationship to his calling. Prior to the event, naming was God's office, but God gives it to Adam in order to be surprised by his acts of freedom. This is an example of *true* freedom—it is an act of unlimited possibility directed *from* the giftedness of God's creation and *toward* God's call.

---

22. Whether or not God grants this freedom beyond the human sphere is outside the scope of this work. I would want to affirm more than an anthropocentric understanding of the freedom I am speaking of, yet I believe that humanity is called to exercise freedom in a different way. There are biblical examples of creation breaking possibilities; e.g., the parting of the Red Sea (Exod 14:21–31), the speaking of Balaam's ass (Num 22:28), rocks crying out (Luke 19:40), etc. The narratives sometimes use language of God's direct action in these events, but must not creation be open in order for God to intervene? Do the stones cry out solely because God causes them to, or is it possible that in the face of human evil that even they break previous possibilities?

23. Pinnock, "Systematic Theology," 124. I am in complete agreement with Pinnock on this statement; I believe that God takes joy in the surprises that creation brings to him. I am just pushing the possibilities of these surprises even further. If God is aware of all the possibilities, the surprise is still somewhat limited—God is left waiting for humans to actualize the possibilities that have already been created.

In other words, our *God-given freedom* is only realized in an ultimately positive response to God. Our freedom finds its grounding in God's gift, and a misuse of this gift will only result in its loss. Therefore, as I understand it, the very definition of libertarian freedom includes the possibility of the loss of true freedom. To choose against God's gift is to choose Death over Life, slavery over freedom, but to respond to God's gift results in finding life and freedom. This dynamic is what Barth points to through his use of "obedience," and what I intend to point to via the language of "faithfulness." Obedience as faithfulness is not a dutiful, one-dimensional "yes" to God's "Yes," even though the response which gives freedom must ultimately answer "Yes" to God's calling.

An example that open theists often use in their defense of libertarian freedom, but which I argue points in a different direction, is the story of the prodigal son. Pinnock writes that this is a parable "in which Jesus represents God as a father longing for a loving relationship with two sons (Luke 15:11–32). The boys enjoyed *real freedom* and were *free to leave home and reject* the father's love, if they chose to."[24] The story is read by Pinnock as an example of God allowing autonomy as an expression of true love and freedom. God has to be willing to allow the prodigal to leave in order for the son to experience love.

However, according to the narrative, what does the prodigal son actually find in his autonomous choice? Slavery. It is not the son's ability to leave his father and misuse the father's gift of inheritance which is an example of freedom, for the son's misuse of the gift only leads to his eating the leftovers of swine. What is remarkable about the story is that the son is welcomed back and slavery does not have the last word. Yet only in returning to the father is the son able to return to freedom.

Once the gift of freedom is possessed in an act of autonomy (and here I am using the word in its post-Fichtean sense), freedom is lost. This is a recurring biblical theme: when humanity attempts to possess the gifts that God has given, they lose them.[25] The first example is the fall

---

24. Pinnock, *Most Moved Mover*, 3. Emphasis added.

25. I am referring both to the explicit pronouncement that one must lose one's life in order to find it ("For whoever wishes to save his life will lose it; but whoever loses his life for My sake will find it." Matt 16:25 NASB), but also to the more implicit motivations involved in idolatry. Idolatry is an attempt to take what is gifted/graced in the world and make it about an economy of exchange. For example, if one performs a specific sacrifice, then they receive something in return (rain, fertility, forgiveness, etc.). This attempt to control the gifts of God is idolatrous because it takes something sacred and

(Gen 3), but beyond that, the theme reoccurs in the Tower of Babel narrative (the gift of power must be scattered in order to keep humans from lording it over one another: Gen 11:1–9), in the story of the manna (if it is kept, it will spoil: Exod 16), in Israel's gift of the land (once they forget it is God's gift, they are expelled from it).[26] Autonomy, in the libertarian sense, always leads to the forfeiture of freedom. Libertarian "freedom" may describe something that we experience in a postlapsarian world, but it *cannot* lead to God-given freedom.

A Multiplicity of "Yeses"

Instead of a morally indifferent choice, freedom can be construed as a "directed response." In other words, freedom is found in responding positively to the call of the loving other.[27] I believe this is the *normative*, or originally created, expression of freedom.[28] However, positive responses can be made in the freedom of singularity; there are a multiplicity of "yeses" which can be used to respond to the original calling. For example, Adam's naming of the animals is limited only by his imagi-

---

makes it about exchange. The Jewish and Christian God (despite some wrong-headed atonement theology) is not a God of exchange. God is a God of grace, and grace is not something that can be controlled. See Herman Bavinck's lecture on common grace for a sense of how the God revealed to Israel and then in Jesus is one primarily of grace rather than exchange (Herman Bavinck, "Common Grace," 39). This will also be discussed at greater length in the fourth chapter.

26. For a discussion of the gifted nature of the land, see Brueggemann, *The Land: Place as Gift, Promise, and Challenge in Biblical Faith*.

27. I add "loving" here in response to Ricoeur's discussion of the divine imperative to love. He asks the question: "Can loving be a commandment? Can love be the object of an order, and injunction?" He answers his question by distinguishing between *law* and *commandment*: "This commandment is simply the one addressed by the lover to the beloved: 'Love me, thou!' But then is it still a commandment? Yes it is, if behind the commandment we understand the conjuration, the supplication, of love insistently appealing for reciprocity. The commandment of love can only come from the mouth of the lover. Only one who loves, but that one indeed, can say, and indeed says, 'Love me.' And, unexpectedly the Sinai imperative ['You shall love the Lord, your God'] rings like the Song of Songs" (Ricoeur, "Theonomy and/or Autonomy," 288). Law cannot come from a lover, but a commandment can, as long as its imperative calls for reciprocity.

28. Here, I am making a distinction between *normative* and *descriptive* language. What is describable is not necessarily normative. My purpose in making this distinction is to account for what we now experience as libertarian freedom without assuming it is the universal norm for humanity. I believe that autonomy in a post-Fichtean or libertarian sense should only be *descriptive*; it is theologically problematic if it is used *normatively*.

nation and his freedom is found in responding positively to his calling to name. His freedom is even further expressed in his revealing to God his loneliness and lack of a suitable partner. Adam's response to God gives him freedom, even the freedom to reveal something new to God. However, in responding against God, he loses his freedom.

In their rejection of God's call, Adam and Eve cut themselves off from their source of freedom and lose their response-ability. In eating from the tree, they alienated themselves from communion with God, essentially responding "No" to God's imperative. As I argued earlier, I do not believe that this was a previously created possibility. God did not expect humanity to sever the relationship, and is surprised by their unfaithfulness. Admittedly, this "No" seems inconsequential compared to the evils that follow as a result (beginning with Cain's murder of Abel), but it marks the beginning of something horrible in creation and in the relationship between God and humanity.[29]

Before I go further, I need to qualify my understanding of "Yeses" and "Noes," because I wish to distinguish between ultimate "Noes" (those which lead to Evil and Death) and "noes" which are ultimately a "Yes" (meaning that they serve life). Particular situations require us to respond "no!," even to God, but they are responses that ultimately open up life rather than close it down. Biblical examples of faithful "noes" include Abraham's argument with God concerning the destruction of Sodom and Gomorrah (Gen 18:16–33), Moses's begging God to spare the Hebrew people (Deut 9:12–29), David's laments, the prophet's intercessions on the part of the Israelites, etc. I would identify these "noes" as the same examples Pinnock gives for God changing God's mind as a result of human interaction. There are certainly times when "noes," even to God, ultimately serve "Yeses." These "noes" may be *painful*, but they are not *evil*. Part of my rationale for this distinction involves an already mentioned analogy used by open theists. They compare God's relationship with humanity to a marriage, and ask if a spouse could not commit infidelity, how can they truly love? I take issue with this analogy, because I do not believe that the possibility of adultery is ultimately necessary

---

29. Fretheim refers to this as the "snowballing effects of sin." He writes that "Genesis 3 witnesses to an originating sin that begins a process, an intensification of alienation, extending over chapters 3–6, by which sin becomes 'original' in the sense of pervasive and inevitable, with effects that are cosmic in scope. However generalizable the story in Genesis 3, it alone cannot carry the weight and freight of the traditional view; the fall is finally not understood to be the product of a single act." *God and World in the Old Testament*, 79.

for the experience of love. Freedom is not found in the possibility of adultery; it is found in the continual choice for the other person.

In a fallen world, however, it is sometimes necessary for a spouse to leave their partner because of abuse (physical, spiritual, or emotional) or because their partner refuses to love them (yet demands love nevertheless). This kind of freedom is different than that described in the open theists' analogy, as it is a freedom for life. Leaving a partner in an abusive situation may be painful, but it is a "no" that is necessary for life. The analogy for the God/human relationship breaks down here, because God is neither abusive nor ceases to love. Saying "No" to God is always saying "No" to the source of freedom and life (unless it is a faithful "no" as described above or as demonstrated by Moses in Exod 32:11 ff.). However, there may be theological articulations of God which have to be rejected in the service of a life-giving "Yes." These rejections may be very painful for a community (particularly one which bases its identity on its conception of God), but it is a "no" that must be proclaimed.[30]

"YES" TO THE GIFT OF LIFE: RESPONSIVE FREEDOM

In my understanding, obedience is ultimately faithfulness to the "Yes of life."[31] Faithful obedience ought not to be considered thoughtless submission to divine imperatives, but openness to responding in a life-giving direction. Faithful obedience requires creativity and demands singularity both from the individual and their situation. It is the openness of faithfulness to a multiplicity of "yeses" and "noes" that allows for true freedom.

---

30. I have in mind two examples: First, the early Hebrew conception of God as Baal that Hosea rejects. When God is being construed as a sexually abusive partner, we must proclaim "No!" Second, the modern conception of God as a determining, static figure who has to be held somewhat responsible for evil. I believe that the community which has demeaned Pinnock is under the impression that he is saying "No" to God, when he is, in fact, saying "no" to a particular construal of God. We must be careful to keep this distinction in mind when we are practicing theology.

31. To give credit to a theologian who has greatly influenced my ideas concerning responding in the direction of life, I must name Sallie McFague and her cruciform ethos which calls us to honor the abundance of life. The following sentences continue to have great influence on my theological life: "The love of God and the love of the earth are summed up in Irenaeus's statement . . . : 'The glory of God is every creature fully alive.' We love God, give God glory, by loving the earth, helping all creatures flourish." McFague, *Life Abundant*, 24.

Following Jacques Derrida, Catholic philosopher John Caputo writes of a "yes more ancient," which "performs (and pre-forms) us before we perform it," meaning that we are always *responding* to this originary "Yes."[32] Reformed philosopher James Olthuis confesses that this "yes more ancient" is God's "Yes," a "yes" to life—a "yes" that both gives and promises life.[33] In faithfulness, we respond to this originary yes, accepting it as a gift, and in faithfulness (as true obedience) we work for the fulfillment of the promise of this originary yes. To God's "Yes" we respond "'yes, yes', with passion."[34] Our "yes" is not a repetition of the "yes more ancient;" rather, our "yes" draws (in response) on the originary Yes and makes it present: our "yes" to life incarnates God's originary Yes. Such a response is the heart of freedom as faithfulness.

Christ-like Freedom

Jesus as Christ not only revealed what it means to be authentically divine but also what it means to be authentically human. Included in this revelation is a living example of authentic freedom. It is difficult to find a libertarian ethos in Jesus's expression, and this may appear to be a strength of the compatibilist position. It seems as if Jesus's every action was synchronized with the divine will—as if his entire life was pre-scripted. The Gospels do not describe Jesus's life as one obsessed with choices where he always finds himself deciding for or against a moral action.

Jesus finds (rather than exercises) his freedom in obedience; in answering "Yes" to the divine call to life. However, Jesus's answer was fully *his own*. This differs from the compatibilistic attempt to argue that our actions are our own, yet are somehow predetermined. Freedom can be expressed in a multiplicity of ways, all of which are truly faithful to the divine call, yet are not limited by God's eternal determination. Each particular faithful response to God's loving call is unique and is the creature's own. In this way, creation can surprise the Creator.

To press the possibilities of obedience even further, suppose that obedient responses made in wisdom have the power to make the impossible possible. What if we were to see the human side to the resurrection in this light? The resurrection is widely understood as a divine

---

32. Caputo, *The Prayers and Tears of Jacques Derrida*, 35.
33. Olthuis, "The Test of Khôra," 111–2.
34. Caputo, *Prayers and Tears*, 114.

intervention in creation, and while I believe this to be true, perhaps we ought not forget that Jesus was resurrected as a *human*. The imagery of 1 Corinthians 15 suggests that it is the humanity of his resurrection that makes our own possible.[35] If Jesus had not been "obedient to the point of death—even death on a cross" (Phil 2:8), would he have experienced the freedom of resurrection? If he had understood the power of *choice* that he had in the garden of Gethsemane as his true freedom, would resurrection be possible today? Jesus makes the decision to go to the cross as a human. If he did not make the decision in his humanity, then we are left with little hope for ourselves in our own humanity. His human obedience serves as an example of the potential of our own obedience. The results of covenant faithfulness can be surprising both to us and to God—in fact, the results can be miraculous.

"YES" TO THE PROMISE OF LIFE: TRANSFORMATIVE FREEDOM

Leonardo Boff offers an excellent understanding of the cross as demonstrative of both Jesus's obedience and his creation of new possibilities. It is unfortunate that Pinnock's misgivings about Latin American liberation theology may have kept him from utilizing the depth of Boff's theology.[36] Boff is better able to argue that evil should not exist because he understands freedom as the liberation from evil rather than the ability to choose for or against it. While Pinnock is able to argue that evil

---

35. "But now Christ has been raised from the dead, the first fruits of those who are asleep. For since by a man came death, by a man also came the resurrection of the dead. For as in Adam all die, so also in Christ all will be made alive." 1 Cor 15:20–21 (NASB).

36. While Pinnock had a period of more "radical" political affiliations, he has since held a very negative view of liberation theology's socialistic tendencies (See Roennfeldt, *Clark H. Pinnock on Biblical Authority*, 120–4). Pinnock writes: "If we are serious about 'God's preferential option for the poor' (to use the jargon of liberation theology), then it is neither wise nor prudent to side with an ideology [socialism] which, as I will argue, has such a bad record in regard to reducing the misery of poor people" ("The Pursuit of Utopia," 66). While Pinnock makes a point about the history of socialism, we should be careful to listen to those who have suffered from the result of the uncontrolled capitalism of North America. We have our own bad record in regards to the poor. I also agree that we must be careful of "self-styled liberation theologians who link the gospel and socialism in a very exclusive way" ("The Pursuit of Utopia," 77). However, we must equally be wary of those who link free-market capitalism with the gospel in an exclusive way, to which Pinnock comes dangerously close.

ought not exist, it must always remain a possibility for both freedom and love to continue.

Boff writes that there are three responses to oppression (social evil): resignation, revolt, and acceptance.[37] Resignation is often theologically justified as submission to a divine plan. Boff calls this "fatalism." He writes that this way of preaching the cross must be avoided because it "ends by legitimating abominations, or representing them as a providence of the will of God."[38] Of this response to oppression, Boff writes:

> Those who simply resign themselves to their unjust, inflicted death and cross reason that, because they cannot avoid the suffering confronting them, they should accept it. These may preserve their interior sovereignty. But they surrender to the cross. The cross emerges the victor, and continues to rend human beings' experience. The resigned have neither the courage of a rebel nor the powerful patience of a Job. Once again on the face of the Earth, truth and justice go down in defeat. Once again the cross has conquered.[39]

An attitude of resignation in the face of oppressive evil leaves little room for hope or motivation toward change. The oppressed are taught to accept their oppression just as Jesus is said to have done. They are told: "This is God's will!" Suffering as a result of evil is said to be the divine method of tormenting the unbeliever and strengthening the believer.[40] While submission to evil is not promoted, submission to God's use of it is. Resignation to God's alleged use of evil is a result of theological principles which have strayed from the Gospel. By contrast, for Boff, Christ does not resign himself to the evil of the cross—he overcomes it.

The second response Boff identifies is revolt. For Boff, this response only answers evil with evil by attempting to overcome oppressive power with power of the same sort. While he understands the pathos that lies

---

37. In relation to the topic at hand, resignation can be understood as heteronomy and revolt as autonomy, while acceptance moves beyond both.

38. Boff, *When Theology Listens to the Poor*, 111.

39. Boff, *When Theology Listens*, 117.

40. For example, as quoted fully in chapter 1, Calvin writes that "because God bends the unclean spirits hither and tither at will, he so governs their activity that they exercise believers in combat.... But the wicked they subdue and drag away; they exercise power over their minds and bodies, and misuse them as if they were slaves for every shameful act." *Institutes*, 1:176.

behind such a response, he refuses to justify it as a fruitful response. He writes:

> The spirit of rebellion may reveal a final human dignity that refuses to accept humiliation. The rebel prefers a glorious death to a shameful survival, and there are many who come to this point of desperation. The guilty ones here are not so much those who stubbornly refuse to yield, but rather those who have forced them to this extremity. Rebellion, however, does not overcome the cross. It succumbs to it.[41]

Where there is violence, evil power structures will remain, and this is the foundation of oppression.[42]

Often we lack the wisdom to imagine the radicality of non-violent resistance, but Boff believes this is exactly what Jesus does in the third possibility. The response that Boff finds in the Gospel is neither of resignation nor revolt. He proposes instead an attitude that finds its true hope in the resurrection. Following Christ, Boff argues that the only response which will overcome the power-structures behind crosses and those who build them is acceptance.[43] He writes: "A third attitude—and the only really worthy, dignifying, and exalting one in the face of death and the cross—is that of acceptance. Death and the cross are still real, still inflicted, still inevitable—but suddenly they are welcome. We see that death and the cross need not have the last word."[44]

It is important that we do not read "welcoming the cross" as resignation; we are never to welcome crosses as just or necessary. How, then, is acceptance different? Because the only way to overcome the power-structures of violence is by transforming them with non-violent answers. The evil of the cross is not to be accepted as a transcendent

---

41. Boff, *When Theology Listens*, 117.

42. Rubem Alves also warns of the self-negating character of revolution. He writes: "Voices from the past had already warned us that there was something wrong in the naïve identification of revolution and liberation. With bitter sadness [Nikolai] Berdyaev had warned, 'It is an illusion that revolution breaks with the old. It is only that the old makes its appearance with a new mask on. The old slavery changes its dress, the old inequality is transformed into a new inequality.' . . . By organizing itself in response to the dominant structure of power the revolutionary preserves, as if in a photographic negative, the very shape of the power it wants to abolish." Alves, *Tomorrow's Child*, 184–5.

43. Boff's notion of "acceptance" strongly echoes John Howard Yoder's account of "revolutionary subordination." See Yoder, *The Politics of Jesus*, 162–92.

44. Boff, *When Theology Listens*, 117.

necessity (part of God's supreme will).[45] It is abhorrent and never used as a tool by God for any purpose whatsoever. Jesus accepts his cross as a loving gesture toward those who build the crosses and in doing so opens the possibility for overcoming the power of evil.[46] Boff continues:

> Thus we find ourselves able to accept [crosses] as an expression of love. We embrace them as a way of proclaiming our love for, and communion with, the very ones who have perpetrated this horrible evil. In this cross we find the strength to experience a healing, a reconciliation with the very persons who have caused the catastrophic wound and breach. This is not a refined escapism, or a supersophisticated transfiguration of the spirit of vengeance burning within us. If it were, we would be bitter. Instead, we love.[47]

Only through acceptance can love overcome the evil perpetrated by the crosses of a violent world.

However, Boff is not arguing that we accept crosses quietly. Crosses are abhorrent and to be resisted at all non-violent costs. The cross is a crime, and it has always been a crime, not least when Jesus was murdered on one. But Jesus, as God, experiences the cross in solidarity with the murdered. Jesus's death made it possible to convert the meaning of the cross. However, this is only possible through the hope in bodily resurrection.

> Without the Resurrection, Christ would be an admirable human being, surely, a prophet who had chosen the most difficult path to tread in the defense of the cause of the oppressed, a martyr who sacrificed his life in the hope of something greater. But admirable is all that he would be. The cross would have meant the end of him. With the Resurrection, the truth about utopia has come to

---

45. Boff does not allow the cross to be seen as a necessary fulfillment of blood sacrifice. He argues that Jesus had to die not because of "some sadistic plan concocted by the Father," but because it "was a historical necessity." The prophetic articulation that the Messiah had to die was not one of transcendental necessity, but because it was recognized that one who lived faithfully to the calling of the Messiah would be murdered by the political forces of their time. *When Theology Listens*, 115.

46. "Cross" is not necessarily literal. It is a word employed to recall the passion of Jesus as well as to indicate death at the hands of one who holds power over another and causes them to suffer. The "cross" can refer to starvation, genocide, economic injustice, etc.

47. Boff, *When Theology Listens*, 117.

light: not death, but life is the last word pronounced by God on human destiny.⁴⁸

Jesus's resurrection is the promise to the poor that they will experience justice. Jesus was "one of the crushed and crucified ones."⁴⁹ He is the hope that those who die nameless will see justice and new life. At the same time, they also are able to participate in creating that new life. The new quality of life experienced in resurrection breaks through beginning with Christ and continues to burst forth in this world through those who give themselves through the work of proclaiming love.⁵⁰

The connection between Boff's response of acceptance and the view of freedom that I want to propose is found in Jesus's creation of new possibilities. Consonant with Ansell's anthropocentric origin of evil, Jesus can be seen as filling the role of the new Adam in a new light: Adam (apart from God) created the possibility of evil and death, Jesus (with God) creates the possibility of overcoming death.⁵¹ Jesus finds his true freedom in being obedient to the calling of the Messiah. However, his obedience was not absolutely determined. The calling of the Messiah certainly contained certain promises which Jesus did fulfill, but he did so in his individual and singular God-given freedom. He answered the divine call in a way that only Jesus of Nazareth (the human) could. His answer was his own, but it was always a "yes" to God's "Yes." We are called to follow Jesus in this very manner: to achieve the freedom of God by responding faithfully in our own singular and surprising ways.⁵²

---

48. Boff, *When Theology Listens*, 129.

49. Boff, *When Theology Listens*, 134.

50. It is important to note that Boff stresses the fact that Jesus did not seek out death. Jesus was a prophet who cared for the poor and healed the sick (See Waltermire, *The Liberation Christologies of Leonardo Boff and Jon Sobrino*, 30). Jesus sought to live as God commanded, and the religious and political authorities had him murdered for this reason. In the same way, the Christian ought not to seek death at the hands of oppressors as the ultimate end to the Christian life. Rather, the Christian ought to seek the life of the prophet and maintain an awareness that such a way of living may cost their life.

51. I am again referring to 1 Cor 15 and Paul's discussion of the meaning of the resurrection as well as Jesus acting as a second Adam.

52. This is in contrast to the pop theology of WWJD. To *copy* what Jesus would do is to forfeit our freedom and reject our responsibility. However, the pithy sentiment may be able to reclaim some religious meaning if we recognize that what Jesus did was out of his own authentic humanity. To "do" like Jesus would be to claim our freedom and responsibility in response to God's call and affirm our role as created co-creators in this world. What Jesus did was break the conditions of possibility, and if we become authen-

I believe this is the definition of freedom given to us by the Gospel. Free will, in the libertarian sense of the possibility to choose evil, plays no role in Christ-like freedom. The moment of a moral decision is not the moment of freedom. Freedom is not found at the fork in the road. Freedom, properly defined, is not the moment of decision between the path toward life and the path toward death. Instead, freedom is found *on* the path of life. Choose life, and choose it more abundantly![53] Disobedience and infidelity, while they may have something to do with choice, have nothing to do with freedom.

Following the path of life leads to ever abundant freedom for all of God's creatures, and even for God. God's ability to work through the faithful allows greater divine freedom and sovereignty, and in this way we escape the zero-sum game that the understanding of the divine/human relationship has become. God does not have to give up freedom in order for us to gain it, or vice versa. Our freedom *grows* in covenant; freedom becomes progressive rather than remaining static, by which I mean there is not a pre-set amount of freedom at the beginning of time which we must somehow divide.

Our admiration of libertarian freedom might betray our North American socioeconomic assumptions. It is for this reason that I turned to a Latin American theologian who approaches theology with different assumptions. This is not the place to hold one set of socioeconomic assumptions over another (and I am not convinced that theology is the best arena for this discussion), but it is helpful to be critical of such influences.

Under a different set of socioeconomic assumptions, freedom is not part of a zero-sum economy in which there is a limited amount to begin with. In such a closed system (as in Kantian autonomy), one must limit one's own freedom in order for it to be shared. Such an economy leads to a limited amount of wealth (in this case, a limited wealth of freedom) that must be fought for. The rich become richer and the poor

---

tic followers, then WWJD takes on a new level of meaning by turning the question back on ourselves. This echoes Calvin's *Institutes* which begins with the following: "Without knowledge of the self, there is no knowledge of God" (1:35). Calvin means this as a reminder of humanity's place before God after the first Adam. However, if Christ truly is the second Adam, our place before God is transformed, and we can trust that being true to our transformed humanity will also mean that we are true to God.

53. A combination of the imperative proclaimed by Moses in Deut 30:19 and Jesus's declaration in John 10:10.

become poorer as the limited wealth becomes more concentrated. There is, in essence, no creation of new wealth, only the exchange of what is left.[54] Libertarian freedom is closely tied to such an economy, it points to a limited amount of freedom which must be divided between God and humans and subsequently between humans themselves. The result is that those who are evil selfishly grab at freedom, ending up with more, and leaving others with less.

Alternatively, we can imagine an economy of freedom which continually grows as it is shared. This freedom is progressive: it continues to create greater freedom as long as its participants live their lives in service toward life and toward one another. The result is an economy of abundance or giftedness which is drastically different from our current form of capitalistic economy.[55] Freedom conceived in this abundance will take on a different form, namely one which does not require limitation. Freedom in the direction of life will be continually generous to all participants. This is the economy of freedom that can significantly contribute to Pinnock's open theism. Freedom becomes genuinely shared and does not require division. It becomes as open as its future.

THE FUTURE OF FREEDOM: OPENING TO THE ESCHATON

The understanding of freedom described above maintains greater consistency between the freedom given in creation and the freedom promised in the eschaton. In Pinnock's model, the prospect of eschatological freedom raised a serious dilemma: either libertarian freedom must be revoked in order to maintain the perfection of the eschaton, or we must acknowledge that the promised perfection might be lost due to the future possibility of evil. Pinnock nowhere seems to suggest that the perfection of the new creation can be lost, so the question becomes how libertarian freedom is revoked. Given the central place of libertarian freedom in

---

54. I am not condemning capitalism as a completely inadequate model of economy. In fact, I believe that capitalism may, at its roots, speak to the openness of creation. For a good example of such an argument, see Griffiths, *The Creation of Wealth*. However, the form of consumer capitalism that involves the ravenous consumption of resources leads toward death. Such an unbalanced consumption not only sets the limits of what is available (because it is not sustainable), but also results in a radically disproportionate distribution of wealth and resources.

55. For a critique of our current form of economy, see Goudzwaard, *Capitalism and Progress*. On page 230, he suggests a more open economy that is similar to the one I have suggested above.

Pinnock's framework, its passing in the eschaton away is very problematic. Pinnock stresses throughout several of his most recent works that libertarian freedom is necessary for love.[56] But if the eschaton is meant to be the most perfect experience of divine love, how is it that libertarian freedom will no longer need to be exercised? This is a question that is left unaddressed in Pinnock's work.[57]

Simon Francis Gaine deals with this problem in detail in his book *Will There Be Free Will In Heaven?*. He writes that the inspiration for the book came from a BBC program that put this question to several people. The answers were split depending on whether an individual prioritized "freedom" or "moral perfection" in the eschaton.

Relying heavily on Servais Pinckaers's *The Sources of Christian Ethics*, Gaine argues that there are two different theological understandings of freedom at work here. The first is that of the early church Fathers, which he calls "freedom for excellence." This freedom "is based on the question of happiness (beatitude) and the virtues."[58] The second understanding of freedom, or the "freedom of indifference," is a result of the modern era and is "dominated by theories of obligation and commandments."[59] Gaine proposes that the dichotomy between moral perfection and freedom only arises after one assumes that freedom is the ability to choose "indifferently." Those who value the "freedom for excellence" tend to believe that there will not be free will in heaven, while those who value the "freedom of indifference" believe that free will must continue.

Gaine finds the transition to a freedom of indifference in William of Ockham, who promotes "a radical primacy of free will."[60] He writes:

---

56. See Pinnock's, *The Flame of Love*, 74–75, 162, 190; *Most Moved Mover*, 4, 12, 29, 45–47; "Systematic Theology," 113.

57. Other open theists, however, suggest character development as a method of moving from libertarian autonomy to a different kind of eschatological freedom. In other words, libertarian autonomy is a sort of first level of freedom that is necessary, but should not be an end in itself. Libertarian freedom is the first form of freedom in what ought to be a maturing process that ends with the individual forming such a solid character that they can no longer "choose otherwise." This is generally referred to as "character formation" and is meant to address the problem that libertarian freedom seems to have no place in the eschaton. See Sanders, "The Assurance of Things to Come" and Boyd, *Satan and the Problem of Evil*, 191.

58. Gaine, *Will There Be Free Will In Heaven?*, 88.

59. Gaine, *Will There Be Free Will In Heaven?*, 88.

60. Gaine, *Will There Be Free Will In Heaven?*, 89.

> Being so fundamental, there were no prior principles from which freedom could be demonstrated: it was postulated as a first fact of human experience. Freedom lay in the power of the will to choose between contraries, a power that resided in the will alone. 'It was the power to opt for the yes or the no, to choose between what reason dictated and its contrary, between willing and not willing, acting and not acting, between what the law prescribed and its contrary.'[61]

Gaine argues that for Ockham, autonomy becomes the normative human characteristic: to be human is to be able to choose. The result of this view is freedom in a vacuum or freedom without direction. In a system which assumes the primacy of the will, humanity is not created facing God, but facing a choice.

The libertarian understanding of freedom is similar to Ockham's in that it is prior to (though, for Pinnock, not more primary than) the human relationship to God. Freedom is thus not indexed to relationship with God, but is a foundation unto itself. The human encounters a choice for or against God upon being created; choice is part of human nature. This understanding takes what we experience now as the possibility of disobedience and reads it back into creation, before the fall.[62] Such a reading of the first chapters of Genesis is not necessary. It does not necessarily follow that because humanity made a choice against God that humans are, by virtue of creation, autonomous decision makers. I believe that a more responsible reading suggests that, rather than being indifferent, humanity was created with an inclination toward God. As Barth emphasizes, *to choose against God* is *to choose against human nature*: it is to be inauthentic.[63]

The inconsistency of a freedom of indifference (or libertarian freedom) is that it must be revoked in order to guarantee the promise of

---

61. Gaine, *Will There Be Free Will In Heaven?*, 89.

62. Pinnock sets up the origins of the world in a way that maintains a dichotomy between good and evil: God was good, the formlessness and void was evil. By doing so, he legitimates his assumption that humanity experiences a freedom of indifference *by nature*. Not all was good in the beginning. In a sense, God had to overcome evil in order to create, and this is in no way biblically suggested. We are not forced to assume that formlessness and void are by nature evil. He writes: "Evil is not even only of human making. Genesis shows us that even in the act of creation God confronted formlessness and darkness and had to establish a life-sustaining order against it." *The Flame of Love*, 74.

63. Barth, *The Humanity of God*, 80.

the new creation. The freedom of indifference must become (or make way for) the freedom for excellence. Once we have reached the eschaton, we can no longer choose against God, otherwise the promised blessing and perfection will be lost. Some suggest that our character has been so strongly solidified by this point that we only make choices for God,[64] but this imprisons us within our own character. The freedom to choose is still lost, no matter *how* it is lost.

Faithfully Open Freedom

A more consistent position would hold that freedom is only ever found in excellence (or obedience/faithfulness), and that indifferent choice is something other than freedom. Pinckaers offers a helpful analogy of the freedom of excellence by asking us to consider the example of a child learning to play piano. In order to achieve the freedom that can be had in playing piano (improvising, composing, etc.), the child first has to have a desire for the piano, and to be predisposed to making music. This implies directionality as the choice to play the piano must come from somewhere deeper than indifference. Then the child must follow the rules and limitations of the piano; they must strive toward excellence. It is only through obedience to the rules of piano that the child is able to develop as a pianist. However, as they begin to master the rules and limitations, they are able to develop individually in the areas of talent and taste, this giving them greater freedom.[65] If they are able to master the rules to a level of excellence, they attain a freedom that allows them to seemingly transcend them.

The greatest musicians have used the rules of music to do seemingly impossible things, to break away from that which came before, yet remain recognizably musical. Freedom, related to excellence, is progressive (meaning open-ended) and requires attentive faithfulness in order to grow into greater freedom. The freedom of indifference can never become more than it is, because it is static by its structural and formal definition. But freedom for excellence is able to transcend its own perceived boundaries as it is always growing.

---

64. St. Augustine suggests this sort of change in his continuum from before the fall, when humanity was able not to sin, to the eschaton, when humanity will be not able to sin. *On Admonition and Grace*, Ch. XXXIII. Boyd also suggests character solidification in *Satan and the Problem of Evil*, 191.

65. Pinckaers, *The Sources of Christian Ethics*, 349–51.

An open definition of freedom is closer to the biblical narrative, and much easier to square with the freedom we hope to experience in the eschaton. Freedom, in this sense, is not lost in the eschaton, but continues to progress to unimaginable levels. This is Gaine's conclusion as well: "I say there is free will in heaven. It is a more powerful freedom than freedom had on earth, because it is a more profound sharing in the divine freedom."[66] Unlike libertarian freedom, progressive, faithful freedom need not be revoked in the eschaton.

I believe that Pinnock (again, serving as a representative of open theism) would benefit from understanding freedom in relationship to excellence rather than to indifference. Not only would he be able to maintain human freedom in the eschaton, but he would be able to rethink God's power. If power is related to freedom (as it is for Pinnock), and both exist in a static amount, then God has to give up power to humanity in order for them to be free. However, if power and freedom can be progressive, if they can be further opened, we can say that God's power and freedom grow with our own.[67] Instead of existing in its final form prior to history, freedom opens with history.

To recapitulate the themes of this chapter, I began by qualifying Barth's account of obedience in terms of faithfulness to the call of life. I argued that the concept of faithfulness better describes the covenantal relationship between God and humanity, giving freedom direction, yet allowing for a multiplicity of responses. I also explored an alternative reading of Genesis 3 which places the full responsibility for the creation of evil upon humanity, rendering God's creation of the possibility of evil unnecessary.

I then described how freedom is responsive to the "yes more ancient:" God's call to life. This response-ability is not limited as long as it is faithful to the "Yes" of life. In fact, our response in freedom is *unlimited* as long as it responds positively to God's call to life, and this is what I mean by *transformative* freedom. We, as humans, are given the capacity to change the conditions of/for possibility in the world: we are able to make the impossible possible. As an example, I used Boff's theology of the cross to describe how Jesus—as the exemplar of our true humanity—was able to overcome the power structures of violence. These two modes

---

66. Gaine, *Will There Be Free Will In Heaven?*, 136.

67. At this point I have deviated from Gaine who believes God's freedom to be at its fullest from eternity past. *Will There Be Free Will In Heaven?*, 136.

of freedom (responsive and transformative) lead to freedom that is truly unlimited. In response to the call of life we find our freedom, and oriented toward the promise of life, we are able to transform the world.

Finally, I discussed the future of freedom: how freedom will continue into the eschaton. Using Gaine's distinction between the "freedom for excellence" and the "freedom of indifference," I argued that we will only be able to secure the promise of the eschaton if we have something similar to a "freedom for excellence." However, unlike most who appeal to the "freedom for excellence," I contended that our ability to respond in creative and surprising ways will not be revoked. Our faithful responses will not be predictable because our "characters have been solidified."[68] Instead our freedom will continue to grow; our freedom will be truly unlimited.

---

68. Referring to the sort of final solidification cited in n. 64.

4

Power Unlimited: Participatory Freedom

IN PRIOR CHAPTERS, I have hinted at the need for a more detailed discussion of power. A theology of power is an important correlate of a theology of freedom. One cannot be free if one does not have power, and all the power in the world is pointless without the freedom to use it (which may well be the situation for a god limited by the logical possibilities contained in a metaphysical system). In this chapter I will address the topic of power and its relationship to freedom, particularly the account of freedom as faithfulness developed thus far. A transformed understanding of freedom requires that we think differently about power, which like freedom can best be reconceived apart from limitation.

The power of God is central to the Christian confession, both as a biblical theme and as a religiously meaningful concept. However, as we have seen, Pinnock and his fellow open theists (together with process theologians) have problematized the classical definitions of omnipotence. They have traced the origins of this conception of power to Greek philosophy and claimed that ideas of omnipotence are the result of the Hellenization of Christian theology.[1] They argue that traditional accounts of omnipotence find little support in the biblical accounts of God's power. Thanks in part to the work of process and open theists, it is now difficult to advocate Greek conceptions of divinity without justification.[2]

---

1. I feel this critique is justified despite a rising rejection of the "Hellenization thesis" by the likes of D. Stephen Long and Robert Louis Wilken (see, for example, Long, *Speaking of God*, 6). I agree that there is a biblical and Hebraic tradition of naming God as all-mighty, and this may well be translated as all-powerful, but naming God as all-powerful and applying the concept of omnipotence are different things. They carry different meaning in both reference and historical content.

2. It is now rare for classical theists to refer to Greek conceptions of power or knowl-

While perhaps not best described as omnipotence, divine power still plays a central role in Christian (and arguably all religious) life. It is difficult to remain satisfied with a mere deconstruction of omnipotence. Recognizing the "weakness of God" may well be an important step on our journey toward an open theology, but there is a legitimate desire for the power of God to appear in this world.[3]

How can we confess that God is all-powerful without slipping into the problematics of classical conceptions of omnipotence? Is it possible to imagine power that does not function in a zero-sum economy? Could God's power be different than the power displayed in a fallen creation? These are all questions that I will seek to address in this chapter as I continue my dialogue with open theism. I also intend to include some of the insights of process theism, which makes unique contributions to the discussion of divine power.

LIMITED POWER: THE OPENNESS CRITIQUE OF OMNIPOTENCE

Terence Fretheim, in a book that I have already noted as influential in Pinnock's development, goes some way toward developing what we might call a participatory view of divine power. In the Old Testament, he notes, the relationship between God and the world is best described as a relationship of "dual agency."[4] Noting that "any relationship of integrity will entail a sharing of power,"[5] Fretheim often emphasizes divine self-

---

edge without at least some qualification. I am here thinking of the difference between H. P. Owen's *Concepts of Deity* published in 1971 and Paul Helm's *The Providence of God* published in 1993. Though both are devoted to providence, Helm rarely makes reference to the "omni" categories. It is not that Helm denies omnipotence, but he does seem keenly aware that these philosophical categories do not best represent the God revealed in Jewish and Christian Scripture.

3. I find resonances with John Caputo at various points in *The Weakness of God*, particularly in the chapter on the cross (42–54). However, it seems that his reaction to traditional accounts of power together with his insistence on keeping the "event" (or "impossible") at arm's length prevents him from offering a more robust sense of power, one which, perhaps, finds expression in the resurrection.

4. Fretheim gives examples ranging from the very creation of the world in which the earth is called to bring forth vegetation and living creatures and humans are called to multiply and fill the earth (Gen 1:11, 24, and 26 respectively) to Israel's settling of the promised land (especially Judg 1–3). What he misses, because of his focus on the Old Testament, is the "dual agency" of Jesus, who only in his humanity (as the second Adam) and divinity (as the Son of God) is able to redeem the world.

5. Fretheim, *The Suffering of God*, 72.

limitation and divine dependence. Thus he writes, "God's possibilities are closely related to the responsiveness of the people and the openness of the situation."[6]

It is clear how Fretheim's work has been influential in the development of open theism, not least in Pinnock's awareness that God's relationship with humanity is not genuine if God does not share power. My criticism of Fretheim's and Pinnock's view of "shared" power is that it places God over and against creation. Creation can effectively cause God to "hide" in the face of unfaithfulness, suggesting that God's power and presence is necessarily reduced as a result of creation's expression of power.[7] The power of God and creation is not participatory in the truest sense, as it remains locked into a zero-sum game. This oppositional character is, ironically, only intensified by the language of self-limitation as the way to "share" power. Either God or creation can have the power; they can "share" it 50/50 or 60/40, but there can be no mutual participation. I will address this point more thoroughly near the end of this chapter.

Pinnock often writes that God must limit expressions of power in order for humanity to experience genuine freedom. This is the general position of free-will theists: one must limit power for oneself in order to give it to others. This is also a general principle of liberalism, from Locke to Rawls. This makes sense of the "existential fit" that Pinnock appeals to in order to advocate for open theism.[8] Many Christians live in a culture whose social and political order is influenced by liberalism and so experience the world as one in which power and freedom can only be exchanged as scarce or limited commodities.

It is this kind of economy that God must enter in the openness model, in which sharing power means limiting divine expressions of omnipotence. It is important to point out that open theists do not deny that God is omnipotent in the classical sense, but simply qualify this by claiming that God chooses not to exercise this omnipotence so that humanity can make genuine contributions to history. As William Hasker

---

6. Fretheim, *The Suffering of God*, 72. See also *God and the World*, 38.

7. Fretheim, *The Suffering of God*, 72. The idea of divine "hiddenness" (in the sense that God's presence might be limited by our refusal to participate in our calling as image-bearers) can be helpful in calling us to responsibility. However, Fretheim is here reducing God's power and presence to a zero-sum relationship that makes it difficult to account for the experience of God's power and presence in fallen situations.

8. Pinnock, *Most Moved Mover*, 153–78.

writes: "According to the open view of God, God is strictly omnipotent, in that *he is able to do anything which is logically possible and consistent with God's morally perfect nature*. It is worth stressing that God as so conceived is in no way deficient in power as compared with God as viewed by Calvinism."[9] However, in order to make room for other powers, God refuses to exercise this omnipotence fully.[10] "In that sense, God limits his own power in allowing us to be free."[11]

Early in the movement, openness theologians believed that power limitation was the answer to the problem of evil. As David Basinger writes:

> From our perspective, to view specific tragedies in this world as the result of a system over which God has chosen not to exercise complete control is more appealing than to view such events as the outworking of some specific, preordained divine plan.... We who affirm the open model need not maintain that God's creative goals require that many people live in the Third World be allowed to starve or that many children be allowed to suffer abuse. We are free to maintain, rather, that these evils, and also their patterns of distribution, are byproducts of a world containing freedom—byproducts that God, as well as each of us, wishes had not occurred.[12]

This sense of the end of theodicy, however, began to fade quickly as the question as to why God does not intervene began to arise. To this question, Pinnock reluctantly responds: "As an open theist, I cannot accept that God is metaphysically limited, and [instead] try to emphasize his commitment to a free world. I am forced to say that God has made a commitment to the creation project that constrains his actions."[13] It seems that Pinnock wishes that he could say something else, but is constrained by need to remain consistent to his own system.

The enthusiasm about power limitation as a way to answer the theodicy question seems to be lost by the time John Sanders makes this comment about God's action taking place in the present (rather than from eternity past): "In the past few years it has become clear to me that

---

9. Hasker, *Providence, Evil, and the Openness of God*, 101. Emphasis original.

10. This is understood to be an expression of God's "kenotic" relationship with the world, one which is, of course, revealed in Jesus' self-emptying incarnation.

11. Pinnock, *Most Moved Mover*, 94.

12. Basinger, "Practical Implications," 171.

13. Pinnock, *Most Moved Mover*, 149.

presentism itself does not contribute much by way of help in dealing with the question of evil. It seems to me now that early statements of openness overstated its value . . . God has the power to prevent [evil], so why does God not prevent it?"[14] In the end, the God who could prevent evil, but chooses not to, is no more appealing than the God who permitted it as the part of a greater plan. It is doubtful that any theology can or should satisfactory explain evil in the light of which evil's place in the scheme of things could be seen as fitting, meaningful, or acceptable. That said, as I will argue later, a different understanding of power would go a long way in responding to the question as to why there is evil in God's world. The key issue is not in the *amount* of power, but rather the *kind* of power that God is thought to hold.

One final note is that open theists are not clear if or when God would choose to violate the self-imposed limitation of power. Some argue that God intervenes when necessary to steer history back on course, while others hold that God never uses coercive power. Gregory Boyd seems particularly open to God's intervention if necessary, and uses the oft cited "chess master" analogy to explain how God knows when some amount of coercion (or, as he would prefer to say, persuasion) is necessary and when it is not.[15] William Hasker believes that God may be able to intervene, but this would be an obvious violation of the nature of God's own creation as one that includes genuinely free beings.[16] David Basinger suggests that God's decision to intervene is in part based on our petitionary prayer.[17] It can be said that open theists generally wish to hold God to their conception of genuine freedom, meaning that God may not intervene in human history, even to prevent the most horrific atrocities. However, because they also affirm that God is omnipotent and able to act unilaterally, special cases allow for the "genuineness" of self-determination to be broken (an example often cited is the hardening

---

14. Sanders and Hall, *Does God Have a Future?*, 40.

15. However, he does write that "the *genuineness* of the gift of self-determination hinges on its *irrevocability*" (*Satan and the Problem of Evil*, 182. Emphasis original). Thus God's intervention must remain infrequent lest the gift of freedom be a farce.

16. He writes: "God does have it in his power to prevent any specific instance of evil. For open theism, however, such prevention would have to take the form of direct divine intervention in the situation leading to the evil, either by a physical miracle or by stripping the human agent of the power to choose evil on that occasion." Hasker, *The Triumph of God over Evil*, 205.

17. Basinger, *The Case for Freewill Theism*, 105–9.

of Pharaoh's heart). Each open theist seems to have a different threshold regarding the point at which God might rightfully intervene.

In summary, the openness conception of power centers around limitation, and as such does not offer a substantial critique either of omnipotence (classically defined) or of the culturally dominant understanding of power. Unlike the openness definition of freedom (incompatibilism as opposed to compatibilism), the openness definition of power does not really break from classical theism. God is still omnipotent, and what it means to be omnipotent is still very much the same. The only difference is God's self-limitation, but even this does not carry much weight. God could choose to override this limitation at any time, and many open theists suggest that there are special circumstances in which God will do so (whether because of petitionary prayer or because history has gotten sufficiently off-course). For a more distinct critique of omnipotence, we must turn to the other main alternative to classical theism: process theology.

THE PROCESS CRITIQUE OF OMNIPOTENCE

Charles Hartshorne

While Charles Hartshorne is famous for writing one of the most pointed critiques of the classical understanding of divine power to date, it is important to note that his 1984 work *Omnipotence and Other Theological Mistakes* focuses more on the latter half of this contentious compound word.[18] For while he admits that classical theism was right to seek the highest form of power and attribute it to God (after all, divine power plays a significant role in why we think God is worthy of worship), the theological mistake occurs when it is a "tyrannical" rather than "loving" power that is attributed to God. By conceiving of God as having the "power to determine every detail of what happens in the world," God

---

18. It should be said from the outset that his later work, such as *Omnipotence and Other Theological Mistakes* (1984) differs from his earlier work, which I would be less quick to embrace. For instance, in *The Divine Relativity* (1948), he writes that "providence is not just the prevention of chance, but is its optimization" (137). His early critique of omnipotence seems to focus more on the former half of the word, and as such is similar to the openness critique, in that it too is a critique of the amount rather than the kind of power.

becomes the supreme micro-manager.[19] For God is responsible not only for determining every detail of history, but also for acting as the driving force (sufficient cause) behind every event, including those that we associate with evil.[20]

Hartshorne has no difficulty with divine power or even omnipotence in a qualified sense. The problem lies in the connotations that this word now has due to its ties with an Aristotelian metaphysics. Hartshorne writes that Heraclitus and even Plato gave some account of change in the eternal, but others (Aristotle, Philo, and Plotinus) stressed a static sense of eternality.[21] Omnipotence, in the Aristotelian sense, sets us up for a mistaken notion that has no biblical or empirical foundation: that power is eternally set and unchanging and that it cannot be shared (this will be discussed in more detail below). In other words, like freedom, power is situated within a zero-sum relationship because of certain metaphysical assumptions. The word "omnipotence" continues to evoke these characteristics, even if they are unintended. I, along with open and process theists, will only be comfortable with the word if it can be cleansed of these connotations.[22]

---

19. Hartshorne, *Omnipotence and Other Theological Mistakes*, 11.

20. There is, of course, a long history of theological solutions to the problem of evil, yet one does not need to spend much time in a church to recognize that there is a great number of people who do not feel that this problem has been solved satisfactorily. This problem and its "solutions" may represent the greatest disconnect between theology and lived experience.

21. The conviction that the eternal could not change went so deep that it influenced astrology and zoology, for it was determined that "the heavenly bodies were unborn and undying" and that "species were fixed forever" (Hartshorne, *Omnipotence and Other Theological Mistakes*, 8). We, of course, now know otherwise.

22. However, this does not mean that I am uncomfortable with confessing that God is all-powerful. Hartshorne indicates the same, suggesting that there are "two kinds of power," one of tyranny and one of love. He writes that "God's power simply is the appeal of unsurpassable love." This is based on Whitehead's principle that "God's power is the worship he inspires" (*Omnipotence and Other Theological Mistakes*, 14). We will address these two kinds of power below, but a comment must be made about Whitehead's principle at this point. If God's power is the worship that is inspired, then it is difficult to argue with classical theologians who confess that any power short of the unilateral, absolute sort is unable to inspire worship (this is the very premise of Bruce Ware's response to open theism in his book *God's Lesser Glory*). Also, if inspiring worship is the extent of God's power, the result is a deadened sense of God's activity in the world, which is arguably the spiritual significance of omnipotence.

Bernard Loomer

Bernard Loomer's published lecture "Two Kinds of Power" has had a significant impact on my thought in this context.[23] Like Hartshorne, Loomer wants to confess that God is indeed all-powerful, but he also believes that the dominant conception of power is problematic from both a socio-cultural and religious point of view. I would now like to look at his critique of the first kind of power, which he describes as unilateral.

Loomer uses the Webster's Dictionary definition as a springboard for his discussion of the two kinds of power and the relationship between them. He writes that Webster "characterizes power as an ability either to produce or to undergo an effect."[24] He finds this interesting because the latter part of the definition is almost never used except in limited scientific or psychological settings. I will address this second sense of power later in the chapter, but for now will focus on the first.

The definition of power that is more commonly used is one that Loomer calls "unilateral." He writes: "Unilateral power is the ability to produce intended or desired effects in our relationships to nature or to other people. More specifically, unilateral power is the capacity to influence, guide, adjust, manipulate, shape, control, or transform the human or natural environment in order to advance one's own purposes.... Ideally, its aim is to create the largest effect on the other while being minimally influenced by the other."[25] This seems a fair and fitting description of Aristotle's unmoved mover or the God of many a theological system. It describes the true nature of the God of classical theism and open theism, even if the God of open theism puts this nature on hold through self-limitation for the sake of a genuine, reciprocal relationship with creation. The doctrine of *creatio ex nihilo* often serves to safeguard the kind of power described in the definition given above. God is maximally effective in the world while minimally affected by it.

Loomer's critical remarks about unilateral power are similar to my critique of libertarian freedom. First, he notes that unilateral power is

---

23. This lecture can be found as the appendix of Bernard Lee's book *The Future Church of 140 BCE*. In case it needs to be said, I am not a process theist, nor do I find the process position especially appealing. However, this does not prevent my appreciation of the valuable contributions made by process thinkers, particularly on the topic of power.

24. Loomer, "Two Kinds of Power," 172.

25. Loomer, "Two Kinds of Power," 173.

placed in a zero-sum economy in which "the gain in power by the other is experienced as a loss of one's own power."[26] This guarantees a deepening of inequality as those who successfully exercise unilateral power do so at the expense of others, increasing their perceived value and decreasing the worth of those that they hold power over. It is truly a vicious cycle that is only reset—but never truly overcome—through revolt.

Second, the unilateral definition of power presumes that humans are non-communal, that power is best exercised over, not with, another. This kind of power is anti-relational. As Loomer writes, "the self is not created out of its relationships. It has its being within itself. It derives its being from itself (and God)."[27] A community becomes a place only to exemplify one's power in contrast with another's impotence. The sharing of communal power is only for the sake of overcoming a competing community (the etymological root of the word community exemplifies this, meaning literally "with-fortification").

Third, and most importantly, Loomer identifies the religious inadequacy of unilateral power, writing that "the practice of linear or unilateral power is antithetical to many of the deeper dimensions of religious life."[28] Loomer, in my opinion, does not go into enough detail as to why this is so, only going so far as to confess that the religious orientation of Judaism and Christianity (and likely other religions) is one of giving up rather than exercising control. However, his characterization of the dominant view of power and his awareness of an alternative definition are very important contributions to the present discussion.

THE POWER OF GOD CONTRASTED WITH THE POWER OF THE WORLD

Human Power

At this point, I would like to go beyond Loomer and the process critique of power to fill out what I believe to be the religious inadequacy of unilateral power. First, in regards to control, I have already discussed how idolatry is at its root an attempt to control the world around oneself. Idolatry is the refusal to accept the giftedness of life that comes only

---

26. Loomer, "Two Kinds of Power," 174.
27. Loomer, "Two Kinds of Power," 177.
28. Loomer, "Two Kinds of Power," 179.

from God. This is demonstrated in pagan attempts to cause rain or to increase fertility. Idolatrous sacrifice was not a demonstration of submission as much as an attempt to manipulate the gods.[29] Participants entered into a kind of economic exchange with the gods, offering whatever was deemed necessary in order to get what was needed. Idolatry is an attempt to control what seems uncontrollable. It is not a relinquishing of power, but a demonstration of power in an attempt to barter for and secure the gifts of life.

It could be further argued that the first recorded sins in creation, the promised land, and the church are examples of idolatry as control. For various reasons, many contemporary theologians argue that the sin of Ananias and Sapphira (Acts 5:1-11)—the first recorded sin in the newly established church—is one of lying, but this is the result of an impoverished reading. Sapphira's sin might arguably be one of lying, but the word used for Ananias's action clearly indicates that he is judged for his "keeping back" (it is, in fact, his keeping back that is his attempted deception of the Holy Spirit).[30] The Greek word used is fairly rare, in the New Testament it appears only here and as a derivation of the root used in Titus 2:10 (there translated as "pilfer" or "steal"). The word in its lexical form is *nosphizomia* and means to keep back, embezzle, or purloin (literally "to hold aloof"). Even by itself, the word does not imply that Ananias was right to keep anything back, as if that were the morally neutral part of the story. The word in the form used here is especially negative when studied intertextually. It immediately reminds the reader of the LXX telling of the sin of Achan (Josh 7), the only time other time

---

29. Regardless of one's assessment of Anselmian atonement theory, it is clear that sacrifice in the Judeo-Christian tradition is something different from that of other religions in that it is not about exchange. Grace is meaningless if exchange is what the sacrificial tradition in the Judeo-Christian religion is primarily about. There are many ways to think about what sacrifice might mean in this relationship, but it stands apart from idolatry in the fact that it does not result in "controlling" the gift or grace of God. God does not "owe us" as the result of any sacrifice, including that of Christ. God's grace is given freely.

30. The problems with the reading of the sin as the breaking of a vow and the support for the reading of the sin as embezzlement is well argued in an article by Brian J. Capper, "The Interpretation of Acts 5:4," 117–31. A greater historical context is given to this reading by Henriette Havelaar in "Hellenistic Parallels to Acts 5:1-11." For a contemporary reading that minimizes the financial component of the story, see C. K. Barrett, *A Critical and Exegetical Commentary on the Acts of the Apostles*, 262–7.

that the word *enosphisato* appears.[31] Achan too is guilty of "keeping back" something which does not belong to him and is also immediately and severely judged. What is most striking is that Achan's sin is the first one recorded in the promised land (immediately after Jericho is conquered), and Ananias and Sapphira mirror this by committing the first sin recorded in the new church (and the only negative event that Luke recounts in this portion of Acts).

Finally, they also serve to mirror the first sin in the garden, in which Adam and Eve also take something which is not theirs to have. All three sins are idolatrous at their heart; they are all attempts to pos-

---

31. A further problem with many contemporary interpretations is the suggested motivation for Ananias and Sapphira to lie about the price of the land. If it is the lying that is at the heart of this story, then there must be a good reason for the couple to lie and risk such severe judgment. It is suggested that they are jealous of Joseph who is mentioned immediately before as selling his land and whom the apostles call Barnabas (meaning "Son of Encouragement"). However, this is somewhat anachronistic, for it assumes that people who were able to give more were praised above others, just as hospital wings or church halls are named after rich donors today. In context, this reading makes little sense as shortly before, Luke recounts that "the congregation of those who believed were *of one heart and soul*, and *not one of them* claimed that anything belonging to him was his own, but *all things* were common property to them. . . . For there was not a needy person among them, for *all* who were owners of land or houses would sell them and bring the proceeds of the sales and lay them at the apostles' feet, and they would be distributed to each as any had need" (Acts 4:32–35 NASB. Emphasis added). If everyone was of one heart and every single member refused to claim anything as their own but gave it to the community, then Ananias and Sapphira could not have been expecting much special treatment. They would have done nothing that set them apart from the rest of the congregation. Not only that, but the money was not used by the apostles for buildings or anything that would give the couple lasting credit. It was immediately distributed for those who had need. If they did expect special recognition, it would have been very short lived. The supposed motivation of jealousy is suspect at best.

A second problem with this reading is that it assumes that the early followers of the Way were acting just as any other religious group would act. However, Luke's account seems to be about what sets the community apart from those around them. If big donors received special praise in this early congregation, then the church would be no different from the religious groups around them (see John Dominic Crossan's *God and Empire* for an example of supporter's names being written on a Jewish building's pillars, pgs. 156–7). It is also ignorant of Jesus's comments about the poor widow donating "all she had" to the temple (Mk 12:41–3). Jesus comments that the poor widow gave more out of her poverty than those who gave more out of their surplus. I doubt that the early church would have already forgotten this story and would have been giving special praise to those who gave more. Either Ananias and Sapphira had no idea what this new religious group was about, or their sin was greater than just lying in order to receive credit. I believe the latter is more likely—people would not have been joining this new group without giving it serious though and feeling some commitment to its principles.

sess something which cannot be rightfully controlled. The giftedness of the garden, the promised land, and the church prohibited unilateral control and exhibitions of individual possession. The power grabs and consequent judgments recounted in each story are reminders that what God gives cannot be controlled. The power that God means for humans to experience and exercise is different than these examples of attempted control. As Jesus promised, one must be willing to lose one's life in order to find it (Matt 10:39; 16:25). Life is a gift, and attempts to control it will result in its loss. Power expressed as unilateral control is idolatry. It is impossible to try to reconcile the power of the world and the power that the people of God are meant to exhibit.[32]

Divine Power

Christ serves as a segue between human and divine power, as we confess that he reveals both authentic humanity and authentic divinity. A model for both human and divine power ought to be christocentric. Loomer reminds us that Jesus lived a life that is difficult if not impossible to reconcile with unilateral power.[33] This was also a recurring theme in Barth: the revelation of God finds its apex in the revelation of Christ, and as such makes it difficult to reconcile the power of God with the power of the world (or "power in itself" as Barth calls it). Jesus exemplified an authoritative power to be sure, but not the sort that could be rightly characterized as unilateral.[34] As Jesus told his disciples, "You know that the rulers of the Gentiles lord it over them, and their great men exercise authority over them. It is not this way among you, but whoever wishes

---

32. The power of the world is here meant to contrast with the power of the Kingdom that Jesus promises, which is "not of this world" (John 18:36). This contrast is related to the one made between "flesh" and "spirit" (for example, see John 3:6 and 1 Cor 15:35–49). The power of the world or the flesh in this sense is not like the power of the people of God because it is self-originating; it is cut off from the source of its giftedness. The contrast is not meant to deny *creational* power, which is given as the world's true participatory role with/in God. "Power of the world" here serves as shorthand for the fallen, misdirected sort, not as a negation of the properly oriented power of creation.

33. "When Jesus is described as being powerless, and as having renounced power as the world understands power, it is unilateral power that is at issue." Loomer, "Two Kinds of Power," 180.

34. As Miroslav Volf writes: "Notice that the crucified Christ is not a Messiah without power; he is a Messiah with a new kind of power—the power of 'what is weak' that puts to shame 'the strong,' the power of 'the things that are not' that reduces to 'nothing the things that are' (1 Cor 1:28)." "Theology, Meaning, and Power," 109.

to become great among you shall be your servant, and whoever wishes to be first among you shall be your slave; just as the Son of Man did not come to be served, but to serve, and to give His life a ransom for many" (Matt 20:25–28, NASB). This was not mere commentary for the disciples, Jesus embodied this reversal of worldly power in his life and death. To confess that Jesus is both fully human and fully divine is to confess that he reveals the authentic power of both God and creation.

Most secondary literature on Barth's conception of divine power is accompanied by a discussion of God's freedom.[35] As we saw in the second chapter, for Barth, God is always free *for* and not *from* creation (and, more specifically, humanity). For Barth it is "in and through Christ [that] we must learn who God is and what the really divine is and can do."[36] Thus, the power displayed by Jesus must be revelatory of the power of God.[37] For Barth, as for Loomer, God's power is and ought to look different from the power of the world.

If we can trust that Christ reveals the power of God (in contrast to the power of the world)—and I trust that we can—then it quickly becomes clear that God's power is not unilateral, but transformative. This becomes especially apparent—as was discussed in the third chapter—in the apex of the Christian story which is the death and resurrection of Jesus Christ. Jesus does not meet violence with violence; instead he meets the power of the world with a power that is transformative, with a power that is difficult to comprehend even still. God's power is nothing like worldly power, which means that we must not simply divinize worldly power in an attempt to name the power of God.

---

35. For example see Rodin's *Evil and Theodicy in the Theology of Karl Barth*. The section on the divine perfections (including omnipotence) is opened with a chapter on God's freedom and love. He states very strongly that for Barth it is "God, the God who loves in freedom, who is omnipotent. Power in and of itself is evil. Real power is conditioned and defined by the One who is powerful" (88). See also Sheila Greeve Davaney's *Divine Power*, 27–58.

36. Berkouwer, *The Triumph of Grace*, 126.

37. This implies an alternate reading of *kenosis*, which Barth does indeed offer. Rodin writes: "Barth develops his doctrine of the condescension of the Son in the incarnation in direct opposition to *kenoticism*. God is free to be passible, mutable and contingent not by setting aside of his deity and freedom, but as the very demonstration of the fullness of his deity and freedom." *Evil and Theodicy*, 72.

As Barth writes:

> More clearly even than the definition of God by the abstract concepts of the infinite, the simple, the immovable to define him in terms of power in itself has as its consequence, not merely a neutralisation of the concept of God, but its perversion into its opposite. Power in itself is not merely neutral. Power in itself is evil. It is nothing less than freedom from restraint and suppression; revolt and domination. If power by itself were the omnipotence of God it would mean that God was evil, that he was the spirit of revolution and tyranny *par excellence*.[38]

God's power is not unilateral in nature—and certainly not unilateral power given infinite and divine status.[39] Barth goes on to write that divine power "does not mean the sum or the substance of all powers. . . . Created powers, and above all the powers of opposition and therefore of powerlessness, are always distinct from God's power."[40] Further, "It is also not a power that cannot endure another beside it. On the contrary, it is the power of the eternal love."[41]

Thus, God's power does not participate in a zero-sum economy. It is not an anti-communal or anti-relational sort of power, one which is characterized by creating the greatest effect without being affected. Nor is it one that is characterized by the necessary exclusion of other powers. God's power does not rely on the suppression of other powers for its own identity or verification.

God's power is identical with God's personality and is expressed in freedom and love. Divine power is not an attribute, but identical with God's-self. As Sheila Greeve Davaney writes:

> [Barth] deliberately chooses to speak of God's perfections rather than the often-used notion of attributes. For Barth, the term at-

---

38. Barth, *CD*, 2/1:524.

39. Calvin also recognizes this, rejecting "absolute power" as an abstraction. As Anna Case-Winters writes: "One could not speak of divine power apart from divine willing. For Calvin, God's power is coterminous with God's will. . . . The divine will, it should be remembered is not being understood in some abstract sense, but in a *personal* mode. It is not a neutral blind force of nature. . . . It has a certain character. In God's case, it has the character of goodness and justice which are part of the divine nature. As Calvin says, "It is no more necessary for him to be God than for him to be good." *God's Power*, 43. Emphasis original.

40. Barth, *CD*, 2/1:538.

41. Barth, *CD*, 2/1:538.

tributes implies or indicates a quality, characteristic, or capacity which is held in common with others. In relation to God Barth rejects any such suggestion. God does not share God's attributes in common with any other being. Rather, they are God's alone; indeed God is God's perfections. God's perfections are identical with God's being and as such "every individual perfection in God is nothing but God himself."[42]

While the concept of omnipotence might rightly point to the fact that God is all-powerful, the irony is that in a traditional account of omnipotence it is a fallen (or worldly) power that is projected onto God. Freuerbach was at least half right. Humanity has used theology to project its own wishful (though, for Freuerbach, authentic) illusions onto God. However, the heart of this mistake was not a human desire to exceed nature (as the 1848 *Lectures on the Essence of Religion* suggests). This desire certainly played a role in theological projection, yet the true shortcoming lay not in the *reason* for the projection but in its *content*. In the projection of omnipotence, this content consists in a competitive, unilateral form of power. In this theological construction, divine power becomes opposed to creation. However, as Barth reminded us above, God's power does not create powerlessness. The power of God is different from the power of the world, and not only in quantity. Divine power is not just the sum or absolutization of worldly power, but is qualitatively—and thus transformatively—different.

So how does a different conception of divine power shape the way we encounter the world? The Sermon on the Mount suggests that God intends to invert the wisdom and power of the world with a wisdom and power of God's own making. First Corinthians 1:18–31 tells us that the word of the cross is foolishness to the world and that God has chosen that which appears foolish and weak to shame that which appears wise and strong. Is this not the Good News: that the world as we know it does not have the last word? If we confess this, then how might we participate in transforming the power of the world with the power of God? This will be the subject of the final section of this chapter.

Summary and Analysis of the Critiques of Omnipotence

As we have seen above, open theists take a different tack than the "stronger" or more radical critique of omnipotence offered by process theists.

---

42. Davaney, *Divine Power*, 28.

However, I believe that open theists undermine their own intentions on this very point. Instead of directly confronting the kind of power implied in traditional accounts of omnipotence, they instead talk about limitations of that power. In other words, they are satisfied with classical theism's definition of power; they just feel that there is too much of it—that the amount of power God exercises in traditional definitions of providence undercuts creation's power and autonomy. This puts them in the uncomfortable position of having to determine how much is too much and why. It also makes them vulnerable to the kind of critique put forward by Bruce Ware which accuses them of limiting God's glory for the sake of human interests. The limitation of God's power is in fact a less compelling rejection of the classical definition of omnipotence than the rejection of the kind of power attributed to the divine.

Critics are rightly frustrated by the seeming double-speak of open theists when they claim that God limits God's own power while at the same time claiming that this in fact makes God greater. Here I think that the process approach is more fruitful because it does not claim limitation, but instead rejects the kind of power God is said to hold. Process theists are able to maintain that God has and is always able to express all of the most perfect kind of power while rejecting the unilateral nature of that power.

Of course, process theists are also infamous for suggesting that God coexisted with a primordial chaos prior to creation. This qualifies divine power from the beginning, making power-sharing an ontological precondition. In the creative process, God was and still is frustrated by the world, which, in its very essence, cannot be controlled.[43] For the process

---

43. Catherine Keller writes one of the most thorough explorations of God's creative relationship with *tehom* (the Hebrew word for what is usually translated as the "deep" or the "waters") in her book *Face of The Deep*. She uses this word to secure the depth, mystery, and fecundity of the world. Speaking to the subject at hand, she writes: "The gap between the *nihil* [nothingness] and *tehom* [depth] provides an affirmative possibility: the chance for a creativity that does not confuse itself with control, for an order that does not effect homogeneity, for a depth that is not identifiable with subjectivity" (6). Creation out of chaos allows process theist to challenge omnipotence in a way that open theism cannot. In open theism, God is only holding back. In process theism, God must necessarily create *with*. In the former, creation is given the freedom to resist God's will by God, in the latter, the freedom to resist the will of God is a part of nature's own primordial origins. I find this aspect of the process position one of the least fruitful both in regards to the nature of God and the world, and am not convinced that it is as world-affirming as purported by process proponents.

theologian, power is shared even before the word go. Most evangelical theologians find this unacceptable (and understandably so), but imagining power differently does not require the kind of ontological grounding that process theologians give, and by no means ought to remain limited to the process project.

Many theologians who are critical of unilateral power differentiate between active and passive power. Both Loomer and fellow process theologian Anna Case-Winters make this distinction. Loomer establishes a dialectical relationship between the two, while Case-Winters privileges passive over active. However, whether the relationship between active and passive power is more dialectical or oppositional, I find both approaches unsatisfactory. The distinction implies that active power is always power-over (the ability to create an effect) and that passive power is power-under (the ability to be affected).[44] This does not get at a sense of power unlimited because it only softens unilateral power (active power) with its correlate (passive power). If we are to hope to describe a genuinely unlimited power, we need to be able to reconceive the nature of active power as well.

POWER UNLIMITED

The account I am developing is one in which power becomes even greater as it is shared, whether it be active or passive. This is a power which, through participation, becomes unlimited. Because it does not function in a zero-sum economy, limitation is not a requirement for sharing. The word *empowerment* is helpful in naming this sort of power, which is active, yet expansive as it is shared.

It is important in imagining a more participatory form of power that we do not find ourselves slipping into language of limitation or res-

---

44. I have not yet explained passive power as Loomer understands it, and it may be important since we rarely think of power as the ability to be affected. Loomer puts this in terms of size or personality. In brief, the more one can be affected without having their identity broken, the more powerful they are. I find it helpful to think about this in psychological terms: the more one can bear witness to or take into themselves without losing themselves (literally having a psychological breakdown of some kind), the greater their "size" or power. This does not mean people who are able to witness great atrocities and remain mentally stable are better than those who cannot, it is not a judgment of value. What this means in terms of the divine is that God can handle creation and the whole of history without losing God's self—that is the promise and power of God: unwavering faithfulness to creation and its events. This idea is discussed most fully in Loomer's essay "The Size of God."

ervation. This is a fair critique of open theism, one that even process theologians are in a position to make. Only by clinging to a particular definition of power must one speak of a limitation in order for it to be shared. If that definition is transformed, it becomes imaginable that a kind of power is possible which does not require limitation: a participatory form of power.

Participatory power—like genuine freedom—is neither morally neutral nor found in isolated abstraction. It finds its source in God and ceases to be true power when cut off from this source. In this sense it is not a capacity created and then abandoned by God, but is only ever realized in true relationship with God and other creatures—this is its participatory nature.

It is important from the outset to note that this form of power finds its source not only because God created it, but because it is the kind of power with which God relates to creation.[45] God does not enjoy absolute, unilateral power while we are relegated to some lesser, but analogous form. If this controlling kind of power can rightly be called sin when exercised by humans, how can we find hope in a God who offers the ultimate expression of this kind of power? As discussed above, both Calvin and Barth reject this kind of power as an abstract, philosophically derived ideal which has nothing to do with the God we worship.[46] Calvin writes that God's power is of no more necessity than God's goodness.[47] Thus, God cannot do whatever is logically possible (Calvin points out that this is actually a limitation), but whatever follows from the divine will and nature, which is only goodness. Calvin is firm on this point, writing that the claim "that God has an absolute power, is a diabolical blasphemy which has been invented in hell,"[48] and that it is "an impious and profane distinction separating [God's] justice from his power."[49]

Barth and Calvin would certainly disagree on specific details about omnipotence, but they seem united in rejecting philosophically abstracted conceptions of power, instead insisting that the God who has been revealed is one whose power is not distinct from the divine will and nature. Both

---

45. Open theists would say this is a choice made by God, but I am more inclined to say with Calvin and Barth that it is because of God's nature.

46. See notes 38 and 39.

47. Calvin, *Institutes*, 1:295.

48. Calvin, *Sermons on Job*, 23:1–7.

49. Calvin, *Institutes*, 1:214.

reject omnipotence as the ability to do whatever is logically possible, arguing that this is misguided for two reasons. First, it is an arbitrary limitation of the divine will to that which is created (i.e., logic and the conditions of possibility).[50] Second, it ascribes a neutrality to power which denies the revelation of God whose character is defined by goodness.

Thus, two significant—though not infallible—figures in Protestant theology affirm a conception of omnipotence that does not fit—and, in fact, directly contradicts—the world's conception of unilateral power: namely the ability to do whatever is logically possible in a moral and relational vacuum. Barth presses this even further arguing that God's power can only ever be understood as *for* creation. Safeguarding creaturely freedom against God's omnipotence is based on a fundamental misunderstanding of what divine power means when it refers to the revealed God. He writes:

> If we understand that God's omnipotence is the omnipotence of his knowing and willing, and if this is a genuine understanding because it has its source in the divine revelation and reconciliation, and therefore if the knowing and willing of his omnipotence is known as that of his love, the problem of competition, from which all the errors necessarily and constantly derive, withers away of itself. In face of the omnipotence of the divine love the creature has never to think of struggling and bickering for an ability to compete. It will never see its own power threatened or destroyed by the power of God's love.[51]

This is fundamental for the possibility of an unlimited kind of power. If God's power is the kind that does not need to be understood in competition with creation's because of its very nature, then it is possible to understand how this power could be truly participatory.

This does require a similar qualification to the one given to freedom, in that true power can only be defined as the kind that finds its source in faithfulness to God's gift of life. Attempts to exercise power unilaterally, apart from its true source, will seem to conflict with the

---

50. On this point, Barth writes: "[God] is the master of his omnipotence and not its slave." He later refers to this relationship between divine power and will as "omnivolence " (or all-willing). *CD* 2/1:544; 555.

51. Barth, *CD*, 2/1:598. What Barth is describing in the God/creation relationship, the Reformational philosopher James Olthuis describes in the self/other relationship as "non-oppositional (or non-competitive) difference." See "Ethical Asymmetry or the Symmetry of Mutuality?" 146–50.

omnipotence of God. However, this is because it is not authentic power. Analogous to an Augustinian theory of evil as privation, alienated power has no origin, no belonging in creation. "Power in itself" is nothingness, it can have no lasting form in the world. In a strict sense, it only exists in the imagination of philosophers and tyrants. This is not to say that attempts at unilateral power do not have concrete effects and a momentum of their own.[52] Chasing this counterfeit brand of power has led to horrific consequences in the world. However, these movements and the atrocities that they produce do not find their foundation in God or in the world as it was created. They are truly nihilistic, finding neither their origin nor destiny in God, but instead in nothingness. They are misguided attempts at obtaining unlimited power for their constituents, but are fundamentally flawed in the fact that they rely on suppressing rather than creating power. True power, the kind given by God, will always rise again. No oppressive force is able to suppress it forever. Because these competitive forms of power are privations of true power, they will always fail. One of the promises of God's omnipotence defined in this way is that it will never be squelched by false, worldly powers.

This participatory form of power can be traced as a strong theme throughout the entire biblical narrative. First, as Fretheim has pointed out, God creates the world in a way that suggests participatory power, calling for creation to "bring forth" vegetation and living creatures (Gen 1:11–24). It is also possible to understand God's "Let Us make man in Our image, according to Our likeness" (Gen 1:26 NASB) as directed toward creation; humanity being created in both the image and likeness of God *and* creation.[53] This empowerment continues in the Genesis narra-

---

52. Brian Walsh explains this momentum in an article on idolatry. He writes: "There is, however, a certain dynamic to idolatry. Graven images not only usurp our proper place as God's image-bearers, they also serve to transform our lives in their own image. . . . Idols may well be human products, but they turn on their producers with demonic power. Once humans relinquish their calling to image the Creator in covenantal faithfulness and give their hearts to false images, alien gods, it is inevitable that their lives will be deformed in the image of the idol" ("Late/Post Modernity and Idolatry," 3). Demonic power is not authentic power, but power alienated from God. This does not mean, however, that it does not have a momentum of its own, but precisely that its momentum is *of its own* rather than from/to God.

53. This may seem like a radical suggestion, but it is not hard to imagine in context (God is addressing creation in all of the preceding speech-acts), nor if one assumes that the "us" refers to a "divine council" which is not a part of the Godhead (this is the scholarly consensus as P. D. Miller demonstrates in *Genesis 1-11*, 9–18). If this account of

tive, as God creates man and woman with the call to fill the earth (Gen 1:28). There is no sense in the story that God's power conflicts with the power of creation or humanity until the story of the fall. God expresses only satisfaction with the forms of life that the earth brings forth, assuming that creation does play a role in bringing forth the fecundity of plant and animal life as expressed in the opening creation account from Genesis 1–2:4.[54] In the Garden of Eden narrative, Adam's freedom is found in naming the animals and is not opposed to God's power or purposes. God's power flows into and through creation without competition. Before human beings take something which is not given to them, there is no sense of matter conflicting with spirit or of creation struggling with God.[55] A unilateral account of God's power in the creation stories would be forced at best.

Even after the fall, God's power continues to be participatory. Granted, now that evil has entered the world, God's power appears to be in conflict with those who attempt to exercise their "own" power in the world (false power, which is alienated from God). In the stories that follow creation (Noah, Abraham, Isaac, Jacob, and Joseph), God continues to rely on the participation of the righteous to enact God's will in the

---

the plural reference is accepted, the members of the divine council (while not defined) are certainly created, making it entirely plausible that God is addressing creation itself. The shift in the reading I am suggesting here does not require substituting creation for God, but substituting creation for undefined, semi-divine beings. It also accounts for what seems to be an inconsistency between the two narratives; Adam is created from the earth in the Garden of Eden account, but in the original creation story man and woman seem to appear out of thin air. If one assumes that God is addressing creation in the earlier creation account, humanity's creation is again connected with the earth. Further it coheres with Gen 5:1–3 in which the language of humanity being created in the image and likeness of God is repeated and then mirrored by Adam bearing a son "in his own likeness, according to his image" (NASB). This reading is my own expansion on the one that Nicholas Ansell suggests in "Commentary: Genesis 1:27f," 24.

54. The Garden of Eden narrative (Gen 2:4–25) suggests that God plays a more decisive role in forming beasts and vegetation, but still does not deny creation's participation in the creative process.

55. I indicated above that I find the process account of preexistent chaos frustrating God's creative process dissatisfactory, and one reason is because this account is difficult to reconcile with the Genesis narrative. Granted, there are other resources such as Job and Psalms which could be read in support of the chaos account, but this reading only serves to give an ontological foundation for competitive forms of power. I would not, as some critics have, suggest that there is no support for the chaos account in the Judeo-Christian religious heritage, but I fail to see how the account gives us a more promising story of origins than one of *creatio ex nihilo*.

world. The followers of God find their power rather than lose it in their covenant participation. In each instance of participation, true power is found, but it is the true power of each individual. Yes, they participate in God's power, but it is given to them to "make their own." Abraham and Jacob both struggle with God; Jacob physically so, earning the name Israel ("the one who wrestles with God"). Neither are condemned for genuinely participating in divine power (struggling with God is not the same as competing against God for an alienated form of power), but are in fact commended as heroes of the faith. It seems that God's power can not only withstand participation, but that such participation is a description of normative (or true) creaturely power.

I hope that it is clear how this form of participation is different from submission. In many ways there is not a great gulf between classical theism and what I am suggesting, but this point in particular separates the articulation of power-sharing given above and from the classical position. Participation in the power of God is not a strict form of obedience. There is room for freedom, space for us to participate in making God's power present in the world. This includes the freedom to make mistakes while genuinely following God's call to bring love, peace, and justice into the world. Luther's infamous sentiment oft quoted as "Love God and sin boldly" gets at this responsibility: "Be a sinner, and let your sins be strong [sin boldly], but let your trust in Christ be stronger, and rejoice in Christ who is the victor over sin, death, and the world. We will commit sins while we are here, for this life is not a place where justice resides."[56] I take this to mean that we can trust that God will be gracious if we are imperfect in participating in divine power.[57] If we are truly oriented towards God's love, peace, and justice, then we ought to feel free to act with the power of God, participating in bringing the kingdom that Jesus promised into our time and into our world. At the same time, this ought not conflict with Jesus' calling us to be perfect as God is perfect (Matt 5:48). We are to strive for perfection in our participation with God, but not to the point that we are paralyzed, left waiting for God to act without us.

---

56. Luther, "Let Your Sins Be Strong," paragraph 13. Luther does not stop with sin, but looks forward in hope to God's kingdom which will be a place where justice resides fully.

57. It is better to err in freedom than to abdicate responsibility. As Paul writes: "Therefore there is no condemnation for those who are in Christ Jesus. For the law of the Spirit of life in Christ Jesus has set you free from the law of sin and death" (Rom 8:1–2 NASB).

The fullest example of participatory power is revealed in the life of Jesus, and if we accept a robust christology, then we can trust that he represents what it means to be authentically human in relationship with God. Jesus was clear that those who knew him, knew God (John 14:7–15). This is because Jesus brings God's power into the world. However, what is even more important for our discussion and for our lives is that Jesus promises the following: "Truly, truly, I say to you, he who believes in Me, the works that I do, he will do also; and greater works than these he will do" (John 14:12, NASB). The example that Christ gives of participatory power is not limited to himself, but will exceed these limits for those who follow him. This is the heart of unlimited power.

The power given to us by God and promised by Jesus is not unilateral in any sense, nor is it power for power's sake. The power given to us is truly God's power. We are divinely empowered to bring the peace and justice of God into the world. This constitutes authentic power, any deviation being an alienation of our power from its true source. Divine power and human power do not contradict. When authentically directed, they come together. As such, we can trust that true power is unlimited, that God's power is never exhausted, and that if we find ourselves in God, we can participate in the power of God.

SUMMARY

In summarizing the foregoing discussion, I want to begin by underlining the fact that my suggested alternative to the openness critique of omnipotence is not one born of a critical spirit, but one which I hope may strengthen the openness position. Pinnock and the other open theists are right to question classical formulations of omnipotence. Calvin's critique of a certain kind of omnipotence was bold in his time, but this is a boldness that has been lost in a great deal of the theology constructed in our own time. It would not be unfair to say that many Protestants think of an abstract, absolute form of power when they think of omnipotence. Pinnock is right to respond to this and to continue to question whether some of the implications of Calvin's other doctrines are at odds with his critique of absolute power. However, the concept of God limiting God's own power in order to allow for creational power is not the strongest position that open theists can adopt. It rightly exposes them to the critiques leveled by Bruce Ware and others; limitation is difficult to reconcile with the power and glory of God. I believe that working with non-competitive forms of power offers a viable alternative both to forms which require limitation and to those (like Ware's) which pit God's glory against creation's glory. It is my hope that this would be considered more of a friendly amendment to Pinnock's work than a competing or critical response.

We have traced the critiques of omnipotence that have been put forward in both open theism and process theology. The openness critique centers on the amount of power that God exhibits in history, while the process critique centers on the kind of power God is said to have. The process critique is, in my opinion, a better starting point. However, this kind of critique is not limited to process theism, as both Calvin and Barth harshly criticize the idea that omnipotence is the absolute power to do whatever is logically possible. What process theism adds is both a distinction between active and passive power coupled with the critical observation that classical theism (and especially Calvinism) privileges the former. While this distinction is somewhat helpful, it only softens active power by privileging its correlate. It is an excellent insight in its critical moment, but in the end makes transformative action (active power, which is at its best empowerment) difficult to distinguish from unilateral power.[58] It is my hope that participatory power is able to serve as a way to account for active power that is not unilateral, but is instead fundamentally relational, transformative, and unlimited in scope.

In the latter part of the chapter, I offered my own critique of unilateral power, building on the work of the Pinnock, Loomer, Barth, and Calvin, as well as the biblical narrative. As a critique of this sort of power in creation, I traced the three stories of "original sin" in the garden, the promised land, and the newly established church as sins of idolatry. In the third chapter I explored the idolatry of the fall, but here added the sins of Achan and Ananias and Sapphira. The texts suggest that these stories are related, and that the human expression of unilateral power is likely one of the aspects that binds them together. Idolatry consists in worshiping an aspect of creation as God, but it is also an attempt to control that which cannot be controlled without being lost. Unilateral forms of power fulfill both of these criteria, as created (and fallen) power

---

58. Loomer addresses this point by turning to "relational power" saying: "From this perspective, power is neither the capacity to produce nor to undergo an effect. Power is the capacity to sustain a mutually internal relationship. . . . This is a relationship of mutually influencing and being influenced, of mutually giving and receiving, of mutually making claims and permitting and enabling others to make claims" ("Two Kinds of Power, 189). However, it is important that a robust theology of power include the power to create effects (active power) and to be affected (passive power), and this is what the process critique has difficultly offering. Active and passive power might not comprise the sum of what power means, but both are certainly part of what power is.

is given divine status in the attempt to find a security that can only be ours when it is received as a gift from God.

In developing a critique of divine omnipotence, I turned primarily to Calvin and Barth, but also relied on the incarnation a true representation of the power of God. Referring to the need for a christocentric critique of unilateral power, I turned to the promise in 1 Corinthians that God will subvert the power of the world with what appears to be weakness and the wisdom of the world with what appears to be foolishness. Paul gives us hope that the power of God is radically different than the power of the world, and nowhere is that more evident than in the cross.

I then gave a positive sense of how participatory forms of power show up in the biblical narrative, particularly in the creation story and the revelation of God in Christ. In the creation story, God's power does not seem to conflict with creation, but instead flows into it and empowers it. Divine power might well conflict with false powers, but it is difficult to get a sense from the creation story or any biblical narrative that God's power conflicts with creation's authentic power. This continues to the apex of the Christian story when Jesus embodies transformative power on the cross.

Finally, I drew attention to Jesus's promise that those who believe in him and his works will do even greater works than these. God's power is not over those who believe, but is at work in and through them. Jesus promises divine empowerment that will take on greater forms that even he was able to embody before his ascension. Thus the promise of the Gospel is not only that God's power will transform the power of the world, but that we are expected, and will be able, to participate in that transformation.

As for the relationship to freedom, this call to participate in God's transformational power is given to us to make our own. We are not left without direction, but the promise and call of freedom is open-ended. Jesus leaves his followers with quite a cliff-hanger. How can the works performed by Jesus in his lifetime be exceeded? When do we exhaust the possibility of this promise? My confession and hope is: never. The power that Jesus promises has no limits. It has no competitors. It is the only authentic power, and as such, is always able to be shared. The more it is shared, the greater it becomes. This, I believe, is the heart of the religious meaning of power, a power that increases, as Paul says, from glory to glory (2 Cor 3:18).

Conclusion

As a result of this study I have gained a greater respect for Pinnock's desire to practice theology with a careful (and ever deepening) an understanding of Scripture, as well as his desire to emphasize God's love and relationality. It is out of this respect that this work began, and at its completion, I hold Pinnock in even higher esteem. He has left a lasting contribution to theology and his humility and desire to continually develop has set a high example for any student of theology.

It is in the spirit of openness that I have argued that Pinnock's understanding of freedom as libertarian is deficient as it stands. In contrast to much of the open position, this account of freedom is not derived from the biblical narrative, but from the world in which we find ourselves (one which assumes a post-Fichtean account of autonomy). Pinnock not only holds to a libertarian account of autonomy, but he makes it necessary for the experience of love. Since loving God and neighbor are given as humanity's ultimate calling (Matt 22:36–40), the account of the freedom necessary to express that love is of central importance. Pinnock's privileging of autonomy means that the possibility of evil always haunts what Pinnock believes to be the "true freedom" that leads to genuine love. This understanding of freedom conflicts with any theology which attributes our freedom to our dependence upon God and which hopes for a eschatologically perfected expression of love and freedom.

Barth's understanding of freedom as obedience offers a promising alternative to autonomy, despite its heteronomous appearance. I contrasted the Barthian understanding of freedom with Pinnock's to open up the possibility of an account of freedom which moves beyond heteronomy and autonomy. I then offered an alternative understanding which qualifies Barth's account of freedom as obedience in terms of freedom as faithfulness, giving humanity unlimited freedom in response to God. Freedom as faithfulness responds to the "Yes more ancient": God's call to life. In fidelity, freedom is unlimited, giving humanity the power to transform the conditions of possibility, and in turn, create even greater freedom. This freedom is then able to be carried into the eschaton, not needing to be revoked in order to guarantee the promise of the kingdom of God. Jürgen Moltmann articulates this hope for the unlimited freedom of the eschaton very well:

> The thirst for freedom cannot be quenched by any partial satisfaction. It knows no limits. That is why even the freedom of God's friends is not yet complete freedom. In history it is the best of all possible freedoms in our relationship to God. But even this points beyond itself to the freedom that only achieves its complete and perfect bliss in God in the kingdom of glory. When God is known face to face, the freedom of God's servants, his children and his friends finally finds its fulfillment in God himself. Then freedom means the unhindered participation in the eternal life of the triune God himself, and in his inexhaustible fullness and glory.[1]

It is this inexhaustibility that a zero-sum, libertarian account of freedom precludes. Autonomy might free us of heteronomy, but it does not adequately describe the freedom that we can hope to experience in the full presence of God.

Finally, I explored the possibility of a participatory form of power, which like freedom, can be conceived as unlimited. I traced the critique of omnipotence through open and process theism, identifying what I believe to be the deficiencies in both. I then gave my own critique, followed by a constructive attempt to rethink divine and creaturely power. In the end, I believe that it is possible to confess that God is truly all-powerful while not excluding creational participation in this power. In fact, I find that there are several biblical examples which suggest that participation in God's power is normative and fully expected of followers of Christ. It is participation in this authentic power which gives it its unlimited character. Its sharing is not a dilution, but an intensification.

I believe that the alternatives to freedom and power that I have proposed in this work are able to strengthen Pinnock's open theism. These alternatives are not intended as a negation of Pinnock's position, but rather as an invitation to open it more fully. An understanding of freedom that is qualified by faithfulness (close to Barthian "obedience") and eschatological openness strengthens Pinnock's open theism in

---

1. Moltmann, *The Trinity and the Kingdom of God*, 222.

several ways. Further, an understanding of divine power that does not center around limitation would offer a strong response to the claims that Pinnock is diluting the glory of God. Below I have listed six reasons that a more open understanding of freedom and power would strengthen and deepen the open position.

First, freedom as faithfulness respects the language of classical theism, even if its responsiveness to, and thus "compatibility" with, God's call is opened up to a multiplicity of responses. Freedom qualified by faithfulness respects the strength of the classical position which recognizes that no gift of God can be cut off from its source, but does not need to be described as compatible with an eternally predetermined divine will.

Second, freedom as faithfulness separates true freedom from the "freedom" of the possibility of evil. As we saw above, Pinnock makes this distinction himself,[2] but fails to take it up in his works that deal specifically with open theism. No gift of God can be rightly described as morally neutral. Pinnock recognizes this, but seems unable to apply it throughout history, instead opting for a development from moral neutrality to moral perfection, or from nature to grace.

Third, and perhaps most importantly, this alternative to libertarian freedom fits better with the biblical narrative. The stories leading up to (and culminating in) Christ recount how freedom is found in faithfulness to God's call and not in disobedience (or the possibility of it). However, in keeping with Pinnock's work to develop an open theology, this faithfulness is not predetermined in any way; faithfulness can be as singular and surprising (and I would argue more so) than unfaithfulness.

Fourth, this account of freedom paired with an anthropocentric origin of evil fully removes God from the creation of (the possibility of) evil. Pinnock understands the seriousness of making God culpable for evil, but his understanding of freedom limits the extent to which he can rethink this issue. Instead of making God directly responsible for the creation of evil, he argues that God only created the *possibility* of evil. However, this does not go far enough, for God is still bound by Pinnock's criteria for freedom. Pinnock makes it impossible for God to create free, loving creatures without including the possibility of evil. The alternative I have argued for above allows God to be free to create freedom without

---

2. Pinnock and Brow, *Unbounded Love*, 112.

evil (or the possibility of it), thus placing the full responsibility for evil on humanity.

Fifth, freedom qualified as faithful and open is a freedom that can be consistently maintained into the eschaton. Instead of losing the libertarian choice that is necessary for freedom in this world, the freedom that we were created with is the freedom that we will carry into the eschaton. This would add significant strength to Pinnock's position, for the eschaton would not require the loss of creational freedom (as it does if we assume that creational freedom is libertarian), but would require instead an expansion of creational freedom. This is how I understand Paul's statement that "it is *for freedom* that Christ has set us free" (Gal 5:1, NIV).

Finally, participatory power gives a sense of how this freedom is given its momentum. How can our freedom come to expression if it were not through power given by God? Instead of demanding that a certain amount of power be set aside for creation's use apart from God, it is possible to imagine a participation of creation in God's power. This resolves the need to talk about God's self-limitation and would enable open theists (and others) to conceive of a limitless power that does not function in an economy of exchange. Authentic freedom would then have its power in the same source, not as a capacity alien from God, but as a gift that can only be enjoyed in right relationship with God.

If Pinnock were to open up his understanding of freedom, his theology would open even further to new possibilities. I believe that we can move forward to a concept of freedom that is beyond the current dichotomy of heteronomy and autonomy. Such an understanding of freedom responds to the gift of life given in God's act of creation, empowering us to transform the world as we faithfully anticipate God's promise to dwell with us. Freedom is given to us so that we might be free, not so that we might risk enslaving ourselves. True freedom is the gift and promise of life without the possibility of evil and death.

Appendix

COMPATIBILIST AND INCOMPATIBILIST FORMS OF FREEDOM

IT IS IMPORTANT TO make explicit the differences between Pinnock and the dominant theological paradigm he is opposing. I propose that his interlocutors hold something in common that is not exclusive to any one theological system. In order to better understand Pinnock's position, it will therefore be helpful to isolate his disagreement with traditional theology as a whole.

In the chart appearing in the first chapter (p. 15), I suggest that Pinnock's open theism may be contrasted, most fundamentally, with classical theism, the latter being made up of a spectrum of theologies ranging from Calvinist to Arminian. What all of these "classical" theologies have in common, I suggest, is that they hold to a *compatibilist* view of freedom: the view that asserts that divine providence (whether predestination or simple foreknowledge) and human freedom are compatible.[1]

My claim that compatibilism is co-extensive with this broad understanding of classical theism finds support in the fact that theologians all along the Calvinist/Arminian continuum describe themselves as compatibilists. This is despite open theists' claims to the contrary. For instance, Gregory Boyd writes: "Determinists often defend 'compatibilistic freedom'—freedom that is compatible with determinism. In their view, an agent is free if nothing hinders them from doing what they want,

---

1. Simple-foreknowledge is contrasted to middle-knowledge, which most Arminians consider an unnecessary explanation of *how* (instead of merely *what*) God knows. For a description of this view and a discussion of its relation to middle-knowledge, see David Hunt, "The Simple-Foreknowledge View," 65–72. Proponents of middle-knowledge see their position as a "middle ground" between Calvinism and Arminianism. For a discussion of this view, see Craig's "Middle Knowledge, A Calvinist-Arminian Rapprochement?"

though what an agent wants is determined and itself determines how the agent acts. Pinnock, *along with all other Arminians* and open theists, does not think compatibilistic freedom is consistent with our sense of moral responsibility."[2]

However, this attempt to associate determinism (likely better described as Calvinism) with compatibilism and Arminianism with incompatibilism fails to find support in the writings of Arminians themselves. Bruce McCormack also notes that it is incompatibilism that sets the open position apart from the Arminian one: "The open theists are self-styled 'Arminians'—even 'consistent Arminians.' But their radicality finally emerges only in relation to the question of divine foreknowledge, a question on which their opinions diverge rather dramatically even from those held by James Arminius himself"[3] This makes them true theological "incompatibilists," something which Arminians cannot (nor wish to) claim.

In what follows I will give two examples of compatibilism, one Calvinist and one Arminian. The examples are taken from the book *Predestination and Free Will: Four Views of Divine Sovereignty and Human Freedom*, and offer contrasting views on the subject. However, what they share in common is a compatibilist account of freedom.

As a self-styled "soft determinist" or "soft Calvinist," John Feinberg proudly defends theological determinism in his essay "God Ordains All Things," but does not feel that this contradicts human freedom.[4] Feinberg wishes to affirm specific (not just general) divine sovereignty, and as such believes that God foreordains all human action, yet does not void human freedom, for the individual is able to "choose *according* to his desires and thus (on a soft determinist account) freely."[5]

Another compatibilist position, usually associated with Arminianism, holds that God foreknows the future without foreordaining it. Norman Geisler defends God's absolute foreknowledge as the biblically sound doctrine that holds humanity truly responsible for their actions and yet maintains God's (traditionally conceived) sovereignty.

2. Boyd, " Unbounded Love," 43. Emphasis added.

3. McCormack, "The Actuality of God," 201–2.

4. Feinberg, "God Ordains All Things," 24. Feinberg even chastises those Calvinists who believe that God's sovereignty must rule out human freedom. Yet he is, I believe, in the minority of theologians who would so readily refer to their position as deterministic. Determinism and predestination or foreordination are not necessarily one in the same.

5. Feinberg, "God Ordains All Things," 28. Emphasis original.

Geisler believes that proponents of specific sovereignty such as Feinberg, John Edwards, and Gordon Clark are "hyper-Calvinists"[6] who end up attributing evil to God.[7] Geisler advocates a position known as "general sovereignty" because it holds that God is sovereign over the whole of history (and foreknows it in its entirety), but does not foreordain specific actions.[8] This position stresses human responsibility for evil and divine responsibility for bringing creation to its good end.

Geisler stresses human volition in evil acts, but insists that God is in control. He writes: "Consider the mysterious relation of God's sovereign will and the culpable, free human choice in the following passage: 'This man [Jesus] was handed over to you by God's set purpose and foreknowledge; and *you . . . put him to death* by nailing him to the cross' (Acts 2:23)."[9] For Geisler, as an advocate of general sovereignty, God knows the horrific evil that will be perpetrated by humans, but chooses to create because God is certain that these evils will be overcome by the foreknown greater good. For the position that Geisler represents, the divine decision to create is not a risk because God knows the future.

There is a broad range of positions in evangelical theology, and Feinberg's and Geisler's only serve as examples. However, as compatibilists, they are not uncharacteristic representatives of either Calvinism or Arminianism. Both claim some form of divine providence (whether ontological or epistemological) which they argue does not negate human freedom. Only open theism, with its insistence that the future is open even for God, unambiguously advocates incompatibilism. Pinnock's disagreement with classical theism—in its Calvinist and Arminian forms—is centered around its compatibilist view of freedom. I believe

---

6. Geisler, "God Knows All Things," 48.

7. Geisler, "God Knows All Things," 75.

8. The position that Geisler calls "general sovereignty" can be further divided by two theories of divine knowledge. The first is known as "simple foreknowledge" and is more often the one associated with Arminianism. This account of divine knowledge holds that God simply knows all things, including the future without knowing "falsehoods": things which could, but do not, take place in history. The second is known as "middle knowledge" or "Molinism." Middle knowledge holds that God knows all future contingencies as well as knowing what an individual would choose placed in a particular world and faced with such contingencies. The latter account attempts to explain how our experience of being daily faced with a multitude of choices can be compatible with foreknowledge. However, in either account of divine knowledge, freedom is understood as compatibilistic in nature. For explications of both views, see the essays in *Divine Foreknowledge* by David Hunt and William Lane Craig (cited above in n. 1).

9. Geisler, "God Knows All Things," 65. Emphasis original.

that this way of framing it helps to explain how open theism differs from Arminianism in particular. The rejection of compatibilism is what makes open theism distinct and is what has prompted such strong reactions from other evangelical theologians.

Bibliography

Alves, Rubem. *Tomorrow's Child: Imagination, Creativity, and the Rebirth of Culture.* New York: Harper and Row, 1972.

Ameriks, Karl. *Kant and the Fate of Autonomy: Problems in the Appropriation of Critical Philosophy.* Cambridge: Cambridge University Press, 2000.

Ansell, Nicholas John. "The Call of Wisdom/The Voice of the Serpent: A Canonical Approach to the Tree of Knowledge." *Christian Scholar's Review* 31/1 (Fall, 2001): 31–57.

———. "Commentary: Genesis 1:27f, Daniel 2:35 and Ephesians 1:22f." *Third Way* 25/1 (February 2002): 24.

———. "It's About Time: Opening Our Reformational Paradigm to the Eschaton." Paper presented at the Institute for Christian Studies, Toronto, Ontario, September 2003.

———. "Life After The Law? Rethinking Truth in the Light of John's Gospel." Paper presented at *Truth Matters: An Interdisciplinary Conference.* Victoria University, Toronto, Ontario, August 18, 2010.

Aquinas, Thomas. 2 Corinthians, c. 3, lect. 3. In Y. M. J. Congar, *I Believe in the Holy Spirit.* Vol 2. Translated by D. Smith. New York: Seabury, 1983.

Barrett, C. K. *A Critical and Exegetical Commentary on the Acts of the Apostles.* International Critical Commentary on the Holy Scriptures of the Old and New Testaments. Edinburgh: T. & T. Clark, 1994.

Barth, Karl. *Church Dogmatics.* Vol. II/1: *The Doctrine of God.* Translated by T. H. L. Parker, et al. Edinburgh: T. & T. Clark, 1957.

———. *Church Dogmatics.* Vol. II/2: *The Doctrine of God.* Translated by G. W. Bromiley, et al. Edinburgh: T. & T. Clark, 1957.

———. *Church Dogmatics.* Vol. III/2: *The Doctrine of Creation.* Translated by Harold Knight, et al. Edinburgh: T. & T. Clark, 1960.

———. *Church Dogmatics.* Vol. IV/2: *The Doctrine of Reconciliation.* Translated by G. W. Bromiley. Edinburgh: T. & T. Clark, 1961.

———. *Church Dogmatics.* Vol. IV/4. *The Christian Life (Fragment): Baptism as the Foundation of the Christian Life.* Translated by G. W. Bromiley. Edinburgh: T. & T. Clark, 1969.

———. *The Humanity of God.* Translated by John Newton Thomas and Thomas Wieser. Louisville: John Knox, 1960.

———. "No!: Answer to Emil Brunner." Translated by Peter Fraenkel. In Emil Brunner and Karl Barth. *Natural Theology,* 63–128. Eugene, OR: Wipf and Stock, 2002.

Basinger, David. *The Case for Freewill Theism: A Philosophical Assessment.* Downers Grove, IL: InterVarsity, 1996.

———. "Practical Implications." In *The Openness of God: A Biblical Challenge to the Traditional Understanding of God,* edited by Clark Pinnock, et al., 155–76. Downers Grove, IL: InterVarsity, 1994.

Bibliography

Bavinck, Herman. "Common Grace." Translated by R. C. Van Leeuwen. *Calvin Theological Journal* 24 (April 1989): 35–65.

Berlin, Adele and Marc Zvi Brettler, eds. *The Jewish Study Bible: Jewish Publication Society Tanakh Translation*. Oxford: Oxford University Press, 2004.

Berkouwer, G. C. *The Triumph of Grace in the Theology of Karl Barth*. Grand Rapids: Eerdmans, 1956.

Boettner, Loraine. *The Reformed Doctrine of Predestination*. Philadelphia: Presbyterian and Reformed, 1965.

Boff, Leonardo. *Trinity and Society*. Translated by Paul Burns. New York: Orbis, 1988.

———. *When Theology Listens to the Poor*. Translated by Robert R. Barr. San Francisco: Harper and Row, 1988.

Boyd, Gregory A. *Satan and the Problem of Evil: Constructing a Trinitarian Warfare Theodicy*. Downers Grove, IL: InterVarsity, 2001.

———. "Unbounded Love and the Openness of the Future." In *Semper Reformandum: Studies in Honour of Clark H. Pinnock*, edited by Stanley E. Porter and Anthony R. Cross, 38–48. Carlisle, UK: Paternoster, 2003.

Brow, Robert C. "Evangelical Megashift." *Christianity Today*. 19 (February 1990): 12–14.

Brueggemann, Walter. *Genesis: A Bible Commentary for Teaching and Preaching*. Atlanta: John Knox, 1982.

———. *The Land: Place as Gift, Promise, and Challenge in Biblical Faith*. Minneapolis: Fortress, 2002.

Callen, Barry L. *Clark H. Pinnock: Journey Toward Renewal: An Intellectual Biography*. Nappenee, IN: Evangel Publishing House, 2000.

Calvin, John. *The Institutes of the Christian Religion*. 2 vols. Edited by John T. McNeill and translated by Ford Lewis Battles. Louisville: Westminster John Knox, 2006.

Capper, Brian J. "An Interpretation of Acts 5:4." *Journal for the Study of the New Testament* 19 (1983):117–31.

Caputo, John D. *The Prayers and Tears of Jacques Derrida: Religion without Religion*. Bloomington and Indianapolis: Indiana University Press, 1997.

———. *The Weakness of God: A Theology of the Event*. Bloomington and Indianapolis: Indiana University Press, 2006.

Case-Winters, Anna. *God's Power: Traditional Understandings and Contemporary Challenges*. Louisville: Westminster/John Knox, 1990.

Cobb, John B. Jr. and Clark Pinnock, eds. *Searching for An Adequate God: A Dialogue between Process and Free Will Theists*. Grand Rapids: Eerdmans, 2000.

Craig, William Lane. "Middle Knowledge, A Calvinist-Arminian Rapprochement?" In *The Grace of God, the Will of Man*, edited by Clark H. Pinnock, 141–64. Grand Rapids: Zondervan, 1989.

Crossan, John Dominic. *God and Empire: Jesus Against Rome, Then and Now*. New York: Harper One, 2007.

Daveney, Sheila Greeve. *Divine Power: A Study of Karl Barth and Charles Hartshorne*. Philadelphia: Fortress, 1986.

Dooyeweerd, Herman. *A New Critique of Theoretical Thought*. Vol. II. Translated by David H. Freeman and H. De Jongste. Philadelphia: Presbyterian and Reformed Pub. Co., 1955.

Feinberg, John. "God Ordains All Things." In *Predestination and Free Will: Four Views of Divine Sovereignty and Human Freedom*, edited by David Basinger and Randall Basinger, 17–44. Downers Grove, IL: InterVarsity, 1986.

Fichte, J.G. "On the Foundation of Our Belief in a Divine Government of the Universe." Translated by Paul Edwards. In *Nineteenth Century Philosophy*, edited by Patrick Gardiner, 17–40. New York: Free Press, 1969.

Fretheim, Terence E. *God and the World in the Old Testament: A Relational Theology of Creation*. Nashville: Abingdon Press, 2005.

———. *The Suffering of God: An Old Testament Perspective*. Philadelphia: Fortress, 1984.

Gaine OP, Simon Francis. *"Will There Be Free Will In Heaven?" Freedom, Impeccability and Beatitude*. London: T. & T. Clark, 2003.

Geisler, Norman. "God Knows All Things." In *Predestination and Free Will: Four Views of Divine Sovereignty and Human Freedom*, edited by David Basinger and Randall Basinger, 61–84. Downers Grove, IL: InterVarsity, 1986.

Goudzwaard, Bob. *Capitalism and Progress: A Diagnosis of Western Society*. Translated by Josina Van Nuis Zylstra. Grand Rapids: Eerdmans, 1979.

Gunton, Colin E. *The Barth Lectures*. London: T. & T. Clark, 2007.

Green, Clifford. *Karl Barth: Theologian of Freedom*. London: Collins Liturgical Publications, 1989.

Grenz, Stanley J. *Renewing the Center: Evangelical Theology in a Post-Theological Era*. Grand Rapids: Baker Academic, 2000.

Griffiths, Brian. *The Creation of Wealth*. London: Hodder and Stoughton, 1984.

Hall, Christopher A. and John Sanders. *Does God Have a Future: A Debate on Divine Providence*. Grand Rapids: Baker Academic, 2003.

Hart, Hendrik. *Understanding Our World: An Integral Ontology*. Lanham, MD: University Press of America, 1984.

Hartshorne, Charles. *Omnipotence and Other Theological Mistakes*. Albany: State University Press of New York, 1984.

———. *The Divine Relativity: A Social Conception of God*. New Haven: Yale University Press, 1948.

Hasker, William. "God the Creator of Good and Evil?" In *The God Who Acts: Philosophical and Theological Explorations*, edited by Thomas F. Tracy, 137–46. University Park, PA: Pennsylvania State University Press, 1994.

———. *Providence, Evil and the Openness of God*. New York: Routledge, 2004.

———. *The Triumph of God Over Evil: Theodicy for a World of Suffering*. Downers Grove, IL: IVP Academic, 2008.

Havelaar, Henriette. "Hellenistic Parallels to Acts 5:1-11 and the Problem of Conflicting Interpretations." *Journal for the Study of the New Testament* 67 (1997): 63–82.

Helm, Paul. "The Augustinian-Calvinist View." In *Divine Foreknowledge: Four Views*, edited by James K. Beilby and Paul R. Eddy, 161–89. Downers Grove, IL: IVP Academic, 2001.

Heschel, Abraham. *Who Is Man?* Stanford, CA: Stanford University Press, 1965.

Hunt, David. "The Simple-Foreknowledge View." In *Divine Foreknowledge: Four Views*, edited by James K. Beilby and Paul R. Eddy, 65–103. Downers Grove, IL: IVP Academic, 2001.

Kane, Robert. *A Contemporary Introduction to Free Will*. Oxford: Oxford University Press, 2005.

Kant, Immanuel. *Groundwork for the Metaphysics of Morals*. Edited by Thomas E Hill Jr. and Arnulf Zweig, translated by Arnulf Zweig. Oxford: Oxford University Press, 2002.

Keller, Catherine. *Face of the Deep: a theology of becoming*. New York: Routledge, 2003.

Long, D. Stephen. *Speaking of God: Theology, Language, and Truth*. Grand Rapids: Eerdmans, 2009.

Loomer, Bernard M. "The Size of God." In *The Size of God: The Theology of Bernard Loomer in Context*, edited by William Dean and Larry E. Axel, 20–51. Macon, GA: Mercer University Press, 1987.

———. "Two Kinds of Power." In *The Future Church of 140 BCE: A Hidden Revolution*, by Bernard J. Lee, 169–202. New York: Crossroad, 1995.

Luther, Martin. "Let Your Sins Be Strong: A Letter from Luther to Melancthon." Letter 99, 1 August 1521. In *Luther's Saemmtliche Schriften*, vol. 15, edited by Dr. Johannes George Walch, translated by Erika Bullman Flores, 2585–90. St. Louis: Concordia Publishing House, 1880–1910.

MacDonald, Nathan. "From Augustine to Arminius, and Beyond." In *Reconstructing Theology: A Critical Assessment of the Theology of Clark Pinnock*, edited by Tony Gray and Christopher Sinkinson, 21–48. Carlisle, UK: Paternoster, 2000.

Macken, John. *The Autonomy Theme in the Church Dogmatics: Karl Barth and his Critics*. Cambridge: Cambridge University Press, 1990.

Marcuse, Herbert. "A Study on Authority: Luther, Calvin, Kant." In *The Frankfort School on Religion: Key Writings by the Major Thinkers*, edited by Eduardo Mendieta, 115–45. New York: Routledge, 2005.

Marsden, George M. *Understanding Fundamentalism and Evangelicalism*. Grand Rapids: Eerdmans, 1991.

Marx, Karl. "On the Jewish Question." In *The Marx-Engels Reader*. 2nd ed., edited by Robert C. Tucker, 26–52. New York: Norton, 1978.

McCormack, Bruce L. "The Actuality of God: Karl Barth in Conversation with Open Theism." In *Engaging the Doctrine of God: Contemporary Protestant Perspectives*, edited by Bruce L. McCormack, 185–242. Grand Rapids: Baker Academic, 2008.

McFague, Sallie. *Life Abundant: Rethinking Theology and Economy for a Planet in Peril*. Minneapolis: Fortress, 2001.

Miller, Patrick D. *Genesis 1–11:Studies in Structure and Theme*. Journal for the Study of the Old Testament Supplement Series 8. Sheffield: University of Sheffield, 1978.

Moltmann, Jürgen. "Introduction." In *Man on His Own: Essays in the Philosophy of Religion*, by Ernst Bloch, translated by E. B. Ashton, 19–29. New York: Herder and Herder, 1970.

———. *Sun of Righteousness, Arise! God's Future for Humanity and the Earth*. Translated by Margaret Kohl. Minneapolis: Fortress, 2010.

———. *The Trinity And The Kingdom Of God: The Doctrine of God*. Translated by Margaret Kohl. London: SCM Press, 1980.

Nietzsche, Friedrich. *A Nietzsche Reader*. Edited by R. J. Hollingdale. London: Penguin, 1977.

———. *Twilight of the Idols*. Translated by Richard Polt. Indianapolis: Hackett, 1998.

Olsen, Roger. "The Classical Free Will Theist Model of God." In *Perspectives on the Doctrine of God: 4 Views*, edited by Bruce A. Ware, 148–72. Nashville: B&H Academic, 2008.

Olthuis, James H. "Ethical Asymmetry or the Symmetry of Mutuality?" In *Knowing Otherwise: Philosophy at the Threshold of Spirituality*, edited by James H. Olthuis, 131–58. New York: Fordham University Press, 1997.

———. "The Test of Khôra: Grâce à Dieu." In *Religion With/Out Religion: The Prayers and Tears of John D. Caputo*, edited by James H. Olthuis, 110–9. London: Routledge, 2002.

Picirilli, Robert E. "An Arminian Response to John Sanders's *A God Who Risks: A Theology of Providence*." *Journal of the Evangelical Theological Society* 44/3 (September 2001): 467–91.

Pink, Thomas. *Free Will: A Very Short Introduction*. Oxford: Oxford University Press, 2004.

Pinkaers OP, Fr Servais. *The Sources of Christian Ethics*. Translated by Sr Mary Thomas Noble OP. Edinburgh: T. & T. Clark, 1995.

Pinnock, Clark. "Baptists and Biblical Authority." *Journal of the Evangelical Theological Society*, vol. 17 (1974): 193–205.

———. *Biblical Revelation: The Foundation for Christian Theology*. Chicago: Moody Press, 1971.

———. "Clark Pinnock's Response." In *Reconstructing Theology: A Critical Assessment of the Theology of Clark Pinnock*, edited by Tony Gray and Christopher Sinkinson, 81–90, 147–54. Carlisle, UK: Paternoster, 2000.

———. *Flame of Love: A Theology of the Holy Spirit*. Downers Grove, IL: InterVarsity, 1996.

———. "From Augustine to Arminius: A Pilgrimage in Theology." In *The Grace of God, the Will of Man*, edited by Clark H. Pinnock, 15–30. Grand Rapids: Zondervan, 1989.

———. "God Limits His Knowledge." In *Predestination and Free Will: Four Views of Divine Sovereignty and Human Freedom*, edited by David Basinger and Randall Basinger, 141–62. Downers Grove, IL: InterVarsity, 1986.

———. "I Was a Teenage Fundamentalist." *The Wittenburg Door* (December 1982–January 1983): 18–24.

———. *Most Moved Mover: A Theology of God's Openness*. Grand Rapids: Baker, 2001.

———. "The Pursuit of Utopia." In *Freedom, Justice, and Hope: Toward a Strategy for the Poor and Oppressed*, edited by Marvin Olasky, 65–84. Westchester, IL: Crossway Books, 1988.

———. "Responsible Freedom and the Flow of Biblical History." In *Grace Unlimited*, edited by Clark Pinnock, 95–109. Minneapolis: Bethany Fellowship, 1975.

———. *The Scripture Principle*. San Francisco: Harper & Row, 1984.

———, and Barry L. Callen. *The Scripture Principle: Reclaiming the Full Authority of the Bible*. 2nd ed. Grand Rapids: Baker Academic, 2006.

———. "Systematic Theology." In *The Openness of God: A Biblical Challenge to the Traditional Understanding of God*, Clark Pinnock, et al., 101–25. Downers Grove, IL: InterVarsity, 1994.

———, and Robert C. Brow. *Unbounded Love: A Good News Theology for the 21st Century*. Downers Grove, IL: InterVarsity, 1995.

———. *The Untapped Power of Sheer Christianity: A Timely Manifesto Aimed at Comprehensive Renewal*. Burlington, ON: Welch Publishing, 1985.

Quine, Willard Van Orman. *From a Logical Point of View: 9 logico-philosophical essays*. Cambridge: Harvard University Press, 1953.

Bibliography

Rahner, Karl. *Foundations of Christian Faith: An Introduction to the Idea of Christianity*. Translated by William V. Dych. New York: Crossroad, 1982.

Ricoeur, Paul. "Theonomy and/or Autonomy." In *The Future of Theology: Essays in Honor of Jürgen Moltmann*, edited by Miroslav Volf, Carmen Krieg, and Thomas Kuchraz, 284–98. Grand Rapids: Eerdmans, 1996.

Rodin, R. Scott. *Evil and Theodicy in the Theology of Karl Barth*. New York: Peter Lang, 1997.

Roennfeldt, Ray C.W. *Clark H. Pinnock on Biblical Authority: An Evolving Position*. Barrien Springs, MI: Andrews University Press, 1993.

Sanders, John. "The Assurance of Things to Come." In *Looking to the Future*, edited by David Baker, 281–94. Grand Rapids: Baker, 2001.

Spykman, Gordon. *Reformational Theology: A New Paradigm for Doing Dogmatics*. Grand Rapids: Eerdmans, 1992.

Strange, Daniel. "The Evolution of an Evangelical." In *Reconstructing Theology: A Critical Assessment of the Theology of Clark Pinnock*, edited by Tony Gray and Christopher Sinkinson, 1–21. Carlisle, UK: Paternoster, 2000.

Swinburne, Richard. *The Coherence of Theism*. Oxford: Clarendon, 1977.

Tanner, Kathryn E. "Human Freedom, Human Sin, and God the Creator." In *The God Who Acts: Philosophical and Theological Explorations*, edited by Thomas F. Tracy, 111–36. University Park, PA: Pennsylvania State University Press, 1994.

Tillich, Paul. *Systematic Theology*. Vol. 1. Chicago: University of Chicago Press, 1959.

Unger, Roberto Mangabeira. *The Self Awakened: Pragmatism Unbound*. Cambridge: Harvard University Press, 2007.

Volf, Miroslav. "Theology, Meaning, and Power." In *The Future of Theology: Essays in Honor of Jürgen Moltmann*, edited by Miroslav Volf, Carmen Krieg, and Thomas Kuchraz, 98–113. Grand Rapids: Eerdmans, 1996.

Walsh, Brian. "Late/Post Modernity and Idolatry: A Contextual Reading of Colossians 2:8–3:4." *Ex Auditu* 15 (1999): 1–17.

Waltermire, Donald E. *The Liberation Christologies of Leonardo Boff and Jon Sobrino: Latin American Contributions to Contemporary Christology*. New York: University Press of America, 1994.

Ware, Bruce A. *God's Lesser Glory: The Diminished God of Open Theism*. Wheaton, IL: Crossway Books, 2000.

Webster, John. *Barth's Moral Theology: Human Action in Barth's Thought*. Grand Rapids: Eerdmans, 1998.

Westphal, Merold. "Atheism for Lent." In *"God is Dead" and I Don't Feel So Good Myself: Theological Engagements with the New Atheism*, edited by Andrew David, Christopher J. Keller, and Jon Stanley, 67–78. Eugene, OR: Cascade, 2010.

Yoder, John Howard. *The Politics of Jesus: Vicit Agnus Noster*. 2nd ed. Grand Rapids: Eerdmans, 1994.

www.ingramcontent.com/pod-product-compliance
Lightning Source LLC
Chambersburg PA
CBHW071502160426
43195CB00013B/2182